CandiD CONVERSations with CONNie

A GIRL'S GUIDE TO GROWING UP

FOCUS ON THE FAMILY PRESENTS

Adventures in
ODYSSEY®

CaNDiD CONVersaTiONS WiTH CONNiE

KATHY BUCHANAN

Tyndale House Publishers, Inc.
Carol Stream, Illinois

Candid Conversations with Connie, Vol. 1
Copyright © 2014 Focus on the Family

A Focus on the Family book published by
Tyndale House Publishers, Inc., Carol Stream, Illinois 60188

Focus on the Family and Adventures in Odyssey, and the accompanying logos and designs, are federally registered trademarks of Focus on the Family, 8605 Explorer Drive, Colorado Springs, CO 80920.

TYNDALE and Tyndale's quill logo are registered trademarks of Tyndale House Publishers, Inc.

Cover design by Jennifer Ghionzoli
Interior design by Lexie Rhodes
Illustrations by Gary Locke

Library of Congress Cataloging-in-Publication Data
Wierenga Buchanan, Kathy.
    A girl's guide to growing up / by Kathy Buchanan. — First Edition.
        pages cm. — (Candid Conversations with Connie ; Vol. 1)
    "A Focus on the Family resource."
    ISBN 978-1-58997-792-1
    1. Girls—Religious life—Juvenile literature. 2. Preteens—Religious life—Juvenile literature. 3. Girls—Conduct of life—Juvenile literature. 4. Preteens—Conduct of life—Juvenile literature. I. Title.
    BV4551.3.W54 2014
    248.8'2—dc23
                                2014026576

Printed in the United States of America

1   2   3   4   5   6   7   8   9   /   19   18   17   16   15   14

For manufacturing information regarding this product, please call 1-800-323-9400.

*For my daughter Jaslyn, whose creativity
and compassion endlessly inspire me.
I can't wait to see the story God wrote for you.*

Contents

Introduction

You may know me . . . my name is Connie Kendall, and I live in Odyssey. I host a radio show called *Candid Conversations with Connie*—which is basically, well, candid conversations with me.

Because I also work at an ice-cream shop called Whit's End, I get a lot of questions from girls your age. And not just questions like "Is there a cherry on top of the Wod-Fam-Choc-Sod?"* I get asked personal questions. Girls feel like they can ask me whatever they want, and I answer from my vast knowledge and experience. (Well . . . maybe not *vast*.)

Somehow I managed to survive my teenage years and actually enjoyed them. I know life at that age can be confusing, frustrating, and difficult at times, but I feel like I learned some things that I could share with other girls.

Girls who listened to my radio show also started asking me questions—and some of them were pretty tough. So, I thought it would be fun to get some input from my friends. We'll talk about God, self-worth, clothes, parents, friends, and even a little bit about boys.

It's a special group—this club of girl-ness. We're funny and

---

* Wod-Fam-Choc-Sod = World-Famous Chocolate Soda

← Yes there is

smart and creative and spunky. We can be sophisticated or play-
ful. We laugh a lot and have tons of questions. We giggle, feel,
dream, and imagine. And there's something about all of us coming together that makes all those things work out in bigger and
better ways.

Can't wait for you to join the fun!

Love, hugs, and chocolate sundaes,

Connie

CHAPTER 1

You Are Not a Can Opener

(But God Still Thinks You're Great)

In eighth grade, I went on a field trip to a factory that made can openers. The factory consisted of a number of loud machines and a big, moving conveyor belt. One machine would pump out a glob of metal, another one would bend it, and the next would add a plastic piece. The glob went on like that, down the conveyor belt, being changed and altered until it came out as . . . ta-da! . . . a can opener. Then out came another can opener, and another one, and another one—until the box at the end was filled with perfectly formed, exactly identical kitchen utensils.

You are *not* a can opener.

But sometimes we might feel that way—as if we're just one of billions of people God made. Even if we recognize that God created us, we still sometimes may forget He *designed* us. We weren't formed out of a mold. He made each of us unique.

I saw how different we are at a recent slumber party, and that's a great thing. We're even different when we eat pizza. Outgoing Olivia likes anchovies, analyzing Emily prefers pepperoni, kindhearted Tamika craves plain cheese, athletic Camilla goes for the mushrooms, and cheerful Penny reaches for the slice with jalapeños. And me? I like pineapple and bacon.

God designed each of us to be who we are. But sometimes that's hard to see. I shared with them some of the questions I'd received on my show, like this one:

> **Q:** It seems like everyone else is good at something, except for me. I think there's something wrong with me. I don't feel special or important. What do I do?

The Bible tells us in Ephesians 2:10, "We are God's workmanship, created in Christ Jesus." My friend Eugene told me once that the word *workmanship* comes from the Greek word *poiēma*, which is where we also get the word *poem*.

Think about that: *you are God's poem.*

A poem isn't built on a conveyor belt. It doesn't look the same as every other single poem. (What would be the point of that?) And its primary purpose isn't to be useful. I mean, when have you ever used a poem to open a can of creamed corn?

Here's a Secret . . .

Sometimes I just imagine God looking past the solar systems that will never be seen by a human eye, the majestic sight of Niagara Falls, and the elaborate colors of the Grand Canyon—to me. And to you. He is thinking, *This is good. She is lovely. With her plain brown hair, snorty laugh, tendency to twirl her hair, big ears—all of her.* Even when there are so many things He created that I believe are more beautiful, He's still looking at me.

A poem is a reflection of the poet. It contains the writer's emotions, thoughts, and desires. And every poem is different. God doesn't assemble you; He *writes* you. And just as a poet thinks long and hard about the words he or she puts on the page, painstakingly choosing the right phrase and idea, so God designs

5

you. Just as a poem reflects the heart of a writer, you reflect God's heart in a way no one else does.

Look at your hand closely. We've all heard that we each have one-of-a-kind fingerprints. But that's not where our one-of-a-kind-ness ends. We also have teeth, retinas, and a scent completely exclusive to us.

So, you are just like everyone else in that you are not like anybody else! You are important and special to God, which leads to the next question:

Q:

Parts of me are ugly.
Does God still love me?

Wow . . . I've sure felt this way. Just today I lost my temper with my friend Wooton. He spilled the ice-cream sundae he was eating, and the mess got smeared all over my new magazine. In the middle of telling him how irresponsible and clumsy he is, I realized I was late picking up Penny for our volleyball game. I hate it that I'm always running late even though I try to be punctual. At volleyball I felt really jealous of Jessica Barnes for being such a great player. I missed every hit—except the one that bounced off my head. So instead of telling Jessica how great she did, I just pouted in the locker room. Why do I have to be so angry, rude, late, uncoordinated, and jealous? How does God love someone with that list of problems?

We all have things we don't like about ourselves—things that make us feel unlovable.

Maybe you have a weird laugh or you get irritated easily. Maybe you trip over a ball better than you kick it. Or you have hair that sticks out and up like you just put a fork in a light socket. You might look in the mirror and dislike your chubby knees or think your ears stick out too far.

But God doesn't make mistakes—and that includes when He made you. He doesn't craft a person carefully and then sit back and say, "Oops. Guess I really messed up this one. Oh well . . ."

God loves *all* of you. He designed you for a purpose. He didn't get distracted and overlook a desired trait. In fact, He's so aware of all that you are, He knows the number of hairs on your head (Luke 12:7).

You are beautiful to Him right here and now. It doesn't matter to Him if you have pimples or hand-me-down clothes, or if you lost your temper two minutes ago. He looks at you with outrageous love. You are His poem. His beloved. And He adores you.

And Psalm 139:13 tells us that God knit each one of us together in our mother's womb. Nothing about you is an accident. And since creating you mattered so much to Him, we know your every day matters to Him. He sees every tear and hears every laugh. He knows you better than you know yourself. He knows if you yelled at your sister or cried in the school bathroom. He sees your disappointment with a friend and laughs at your jokes. No one, not even your best friend, knows you like God knows you. And you can't even imagine the love He has for you. The Bible describes it as lavish, unending, and indescribable. (Here are just a few of those verses: 1 John 3:1; Psalm 139:1–6; Psalm 31:16; Psalm 32:10; and Ephesians 3:17–19. For more, google the words "Bible verses on God's love.")

Penny's Corner

I work at an art gallery run by Jacques Henri. One day Jacques came into the room. He was very excited. I thought he was going to tell me to stop breathing on the paintings like he usually does. But instead he told me he'd just heard on the news that a long-lost painting by Claude Monet had been discovered.

"What's it look like?" I asked.

"I don't know," Henri said in his French accent.

"How much is it worth?"

"Millions, I'm sure! A find like zat is priceless!"

I was confused. "But how can you say that without even seeing the painting?"

"Zee painting is priceless because zee artist is *magnifique!*"

That's how it is with us. We're invaluable because our Artist is beyond compare. You are extraordinary simply because you are designed by the God of the universe.

Troubles with Trixie

Some Bible translations of Ephesians 2:10 use the word *masterpiece* instead of *workmanship*. I kind of like the idea of being God's masterpiece. It means we are unique and valuable.

But here's where the problem comes in . . .

Satan doesn't want you to feel unique or valuable. He doesn't want you to realize how deeply God cares for you and loves you. So the devil is going to try to remind you that you're not good at certain things, that you don't look perfect, that you tripped in the cafeteria and everybody laughed. He's also going to try to convince you that you're not as good as someone else—that you're somehow less valuable.

This problem showed up for me in the form of Trixie Greenwald.

Trixie has beautiful raven-black hair, stars in all the school musicals, and is a champion pole-vaulter. She is friendly, happy, and popular. Obviously, if I were like her, I'd be all those things too.

Or so I thought.

I dyed my hair black, took singing lessons, and went out for the track team so I could learn how to pole-vault. But the black hair made me look like a mortician, my singing instructor said I was more off-key than a kazoo, and my pole-vaulting was more like pole-falling-flat-on-my-face. My friend Mr. Whittaker came up to me one day after a track meet.

"Connie, do you even *like* pole-vaulting?" (He was kind enough not to mention my hair.)

And, the truth was, I didn't. I liked doing my radio show, directing plays, writing stories, and teasing my friend Eugene. That's the way God made me.

"The world already has a Trixie Greenwald," Whit told me. "What it needs is a Connie Kendall."

He was right, of course. And I went back to just being Connie—exactly who I was meant to be. (Unfortunately, it took another six months for my hair to return to being Connie.)

So if you ever want to be like a Trixie Greenwald, tell yourself, "That's not the way God designed me." And forget the pole-vaulting.

Your Turn

Look up the following verses. What does each one tell you about how God thinks of you?

- Romans 8:38–39

    Hint: you are deeply and completely loved.

- John 3:16

    Hint: He loved you so much He died for you.

- Song of Songs 4:1

    Hint: He thinks you're beautiful.

- Zephaniah 3:17

    Hint: He rejoices over you.

- Psalm 139:16

    Hint: He wrote down every day of your life.

Think about the unique traits God gave you. Write down some things you like about yourself. If you have trouble, ask a friend or family member to share what he or she likes about you. Sometimes we don't notice the great things about ourselves.

_____

_____

_____

_____

_____

Thank God for making you with all of these gifts.

_____

_____

_____

_____

_____

Why Cake Sometimes Tastes Disgusting

(Recognizing Your Hidden Talents)

Last summer, Wooton came by Whit's End carrying an absolutely delicious-looking cake. It smelled amazing, like almond and vanilla and cinnamon goodness. I was anxious to dig in and take a bite, but Wooton kept talking and talking. It was all about how much work the cake was to make, how he'd tried different recipes, blah, blah, blah. All I could think of was how wonderful that cake smelled. To be honest, I was so distracted by the smell of the cake, I didn't even hear what he was saying. Well, that is, I didn't hear anything until he said, "So, it's all yours."

"All . . . mine? I get the whole thing?" I was already tasting it in my imagination.

"Sure," Wooton said. "I just want your honest feedback after you try it. I'll come back tomorrow."

"Absolutely. Yes. Of course!"

Wooton left, and I dug out a fork. I didn't even bother with a plate but speared a giant bite and shoved it in my mouth, preparing for bliss. And it was . . . the worst thing I've ever eaten.

I spit the bite out in the trash. I couldn't believe how awful it tasted—like soap mixed with grass and Play-Doh. Really, *really* disgusting.

After hiding the cake in the back of a kitchen cabinet (I didn't want anyone else to get poisoned), I headed home. My stomach hurt all night. How was I going to tell Wooton that the cake he'd worked so hard on was absolutely terrible?

The next morning when I went into the kitchen, the whole place smelled wonderful. So wonderful, in fact, that I wondered if I'd been wrong. Maybe the cake wasn't so bad. I took a tiny, tiny bite.

Yechhh! Nope . . . the cake tasted even worse than I remembered.

I had to tell Wooton the truth. Otherwise, I'd be spending my life eating his awful cakes.

The ding from the front door opening and a familiar "Connie!" told me Wooton had arrived.

I emerged from the kitchen, a smile plastered on my face. "Hi, Wooton!"

"So?" He eagerly sat down at the counter. "What did you think?"

"Well . . . are you sure you followed the recipe exactly?"

He shook his head. "I told you yesterday. I made the whole thing up myself."

Well, that explains it, I thought.

"I'm going to be honest," I said, taking a deep breath. "It wasn't good."

His face fell. "Aw, man. Did it stink, or was it just too bland?"

"It stank. Well," I corrected myself, "it actually smelled really good, but the taste stunk."

"The taste?" Wooton asked. "Why would you taste it?"

I was thoroughly confused. "Because it was a cake, of course."

"No, I explained this yesterday. It's a room deodorizer!"

I remembered the heavenly smell of the kitchen this morning.

"Oooh! Wooton!" I exclaimed. "It's amazing!"

I'd been eating a room deodorizer! Which, among other things, was made of soap, grass, and Play-Doh. Of course.

This incident made me think of a question a girl asked me at Whit's End:

I don't feel like I'm good at anything. How can God use me?

First I told her about the can-opener factory. Then I explained that she might be thinking she's a vanilla-cinnamon cake, and instead she is more suited to be like Wooton's room deodorizer, something wonderful but not exactly cake.

In the last chapter, we discussed a verse—Ephesians 2:10—that talks about our being God's poem or masterpiece. Well, that's not where the verse ends. Here's the whole thing: "We are God's workmanship, created in Christ Jesus to do good works, which God prepared in advance for us to do."

Think about what that means. God has a plan for you. He knew the things He had for you to do before you were even born. He's not digging around trying to find something to fill your eighty years on earth. It's *already* a part of your story. It's *already* mapped out.

That concept might seem a little out there, so let's look at a real-life example. Olivia came into Whit's End the other day and slumped into a seat at the counter. She let out a huge sigh. I looked up from the banana split I was putting together for myself.

"What's wrong?" I asked.

"I can't do anything right," she moaned. "I need to give up trying."

"What happened?"

"What *didn't* happen?" Olivia dropped her forehead into her hands. "It started at cheerleading tryouts this morning when I fell off the stage during my very shaky cartwheel."

"Ooh. Sorry." I pushed the banana split her way. She obviously needed it more than I did.

"Then, in first-period science class, we got our unit tests back. I had studied really hard for it."

"I remember that day," I said. "You came in here with a whole bunch of books."

"But I got only a D." She took a big bite of ice cream and continued. "After lunch, I had band class. I took up the French horn a couple months ago."

I nodded. "And . . . ?"

"I sounded like a whale who stubbed her fin. Painful."

"I'm sure it wasn't that bad."

Olivia shook her head. "The band instructor—after he took out his earplugs—told me that not everyone's musically gifted. He said maybe I should try drama instead."

"Oh. Well, that's an idea," I said with as much optimism as I could muster.

"Sure. I'd planned on trying out for the school play after school today anyway."

"Great! How did that go?"

She shook her head. "I got so nervous that it felt like my tongue was three times its normal size. Mrs. Platt asked me to spit out my gum and try again. Except, I didn't have gum."

"Oh no. What did you do?"

"I burst into tears and, well, came here." She bit her quivering lip. "Connie, I just want to be good at something. *One thing*."

I know how she felt. You should see me play basketball. You might not even recognize which sport it is! And when I took up baton twirling in the marching band, I actually knocked one of the tuba players unconscious.

But Hebrews 13:21 tells us that God will "equip you with everything good for doing his will." That means He will give you whatever you need—talents, skills, opportunities—to do the things He's planned for you to do!

Sometimes we recognize these talents right away. Maybe there's an activity you're drawn to. Pay attention to that. At age twelve, Amadeus Mozart wrote his first symphony. Pablo Picasso enrolled in art school by the time he turned sixteen. As a young child, Frank Gehry used wood scraps to build intricate models on

WHY CAKE SOMETIMES TASTES DISGUSTING

the living-room floor. He grew up to be a well-known architect. Some kids know what their gifts are early on in life.

But finding a talent early is not always the case. Other times, talents reveal themselves later. Henri Matisse, another famous artist, didn't realize he loved painting until he was in his twenties and was recovering from the flu. In an attempt to cheer him up, Henri's mother gave him some paints to play around with. Henri left his job as a clerk at a law office to pursue painting, and he never looked back.

Talents and callings can also be revealed through experiences—good and bad. John Wilson was performing a routine science experiment at school when a giant explosion occurred. A distracted lab assistant had made a labeling mistake, and instead of heating a flask of water, John fired up a container with a volatile chemical. John woke up in the hospital, blinded for life.

That was tragic, but what would have been even more tragic is if John had allowed himself to become bitter and hard-hearted. But instead, he grew more compassionate toward others inflicted with that disability. He heard about an area in Africa where a large section of the population was blind due to a disease passed through an insect bite. John worked with a team to develop a medicine to keep people from getting the disease. The medicine proved effective, and today generations of children can thank John Wilson for their ability to see.

But God doesn't always use tragedies in that way. Sometimes a good experience sparks in us a new desire or a tug at our hearts. It might be the inspiration of a teacher, a service project, a magazine article, or a visit to another country.

Here's a Secret . . .

You might need to simply keep practicing—maybe you *are* a cake and *not* a room deodorizer. We think that just because we're not good at something immediately, we'll never be good at it. But the truth is, most things take practice. Remember the story I told you about Olivia's bad day? Well, she really liked playing the French horn, and so she decided to keep working at it even though it wasn't as easy as she'd hoped. And now she's sitting first chair—and her band instructor threw away the earplugs. She also auditioned a few months later for the next school play. Olivia wasn't as nervous this time, and she ended up getting a part! Sometimes finding our gifts isn't about trying everything until we find one thing that we're good at, but it's about persevering (trying again and again and again) in something we enjoy.

Claude Monet would never have learned he was a talented artist if all he thought about was how bad he was at the high jump. Ludwig von Beethoven might never have composed his amazing works if he had spent his time complaining about how awkward he felt in groups of people. Abraham Lincoln might never have known what a good leader he was if he had never gotten past how off-key he sounded when he sang in the shower.

Your Turn

So, for fun, we're going to try a few exercises. Don't worry . . . you won't need your gym shoes for these. Simply answer the following questions as honestly as you can by checking the box if the description matches you.

1. Among your group of friends, you're known as the one who . . .
   - ☐ never fails to crack a joke and get everyone laughing.
   - ☐ organizes and plans what the group is going to do on Saturday.
   - ☐ is a great listener and encourager. They call you whenever they're feeling bummed out.
   - ☐ can be counted on to have a great idea.
   - ☐ mends the relationships when two of your friends are angry with each other.

2. When you have an hour to yourself, you'll most likely be found . . .

- [ ] writing a story.
- [ ] cleaning up the kitchen to surprise your mom.
- [ ] reading up more on the Civil War. History class sparked your interest.
- [ ] outside practicing basketball in the driveway.
- [ ] taking a bunch of pictures of your dog.

3. In school, your favorite thing is . . .

- [ ] foreign language class.
- [ ] getting everyone excited about a big pep rally.
- [ ] days when a science experiment is scheduled.
- [ ] tryouts for the school play.
- [ ] organizing games at recess.

4. Your ideal vacation would be . . .

- [ ] spending time with your family playing on the beach.
- [ ] building a school for impoverished kids in Africa.
- [ ] going skydiving with your friends.
- [ ] biking across the country.
- [ ] sitting on the deck of a cruise ship and writing poetry.

5. You see a new girl in the cafeteria, so you . . .

☐ invite her to join the Save the Environment Club you just started.

☐ interview her for an article in the school newspaper.

☐ end up talking to her for half an hour and finding out her life story.

☐ introduce her to as many people as you can. Her new best friend is here somewhere.

☐ write her a note saying that you're glad she's at this school, and she can always come to you if she's feeling down.

Take a look at which boxes you checked. There is no *right* answer for any of them. Every single answer indicates a potential talent or gift. Sometimes we get stuck on talents being about athletics or music or art. But being a risk taker, a good listener, or a leader are all-important talents. The person who can make someone laugh is just as important as the one who can patiently tutor her friend in math, and that's just as important as the person who befriends the new girl. It's as necessary to have the person who sees the positive spin on everything ("running a marathon together will be so much fun") as the one who thinks through the logic of it all ("but we need to start practicing right away, and that's going to take a lot of discipline").

We might look at other people and wish we had their talents.

Personally, I'd rather win one of those singing competitions on TV and spend the rest of my days performing on a stage in front of a million adoring fans. But that's not how God gifted me. Instead, I'm a pretty good writer and organizer, and I'm great at getting people excited about events.

One time when Mr. Parker was in the hospital with a broken leg, we all wanted to help in some way. Wooton went to visit him and tell stories, making Mr. Parker laugh despite how down in the dumps he felt. Penny made a gigantic card for all the kids at Whit's End to sign. Eugene built some ramps at the Parker home, so once Mr. Parker came home, he'd be able to get around easier in his wheelchair. And I organized a sign-up for ways to help out the family: bringing meals, mowing the lawn, fixing a broken window. But think if we all had the same gift of telling stories. Mr. Parker's room would have been very loud and chaotic with all of us trying to cheer him up—and nothing else would have gotten done. Instead, we were each able to use our gifts to help in a variety of ways.

So, with that in mind, check any of the following that might describe you:

- ☐ I enjoy playing a musical instrument.
- ☐ I'm artistic.
- ☐ I come up with ideas.
- ☐ I make people laugh.
- ☐ I like telling people about Jesus.

- ❏ My friends think I'm strange because I like to organize my locker.
- ❏ I'm a good listener.
- ❏ I feel compassion for people who are hurting.
- ❏ If I see someone struggling, I help him or her.
- ❏ I'm athletic.
- ❏ I remember to pray for other people often.
- ❏ I don't give up on things; I keep trying.
- ❏ I do well in most subjects at school.
- ❏ I try to encourage people when they're discouraged.
- ❏ I write poetry.
- ❏ I sometimes make up stories.
- ❏ I like to teach people how to do things.
- ❏ I'm willing to try new things.
- ❏ I can catch on to foreign languages pretty easily.
- ❏ I've memorized several Bible verses.
- ❏ Little kids like to play with me.
- ❏ I think up new inventions.
- ❏ I like to sing.
- ❏ I like to bake or cook things.
- ❏ I inspire people to do things. I'm a leader.
- ❏ I'm good at solving problems.
- ❏ It seems like I'm always helping people with their computer problems.

☐ Animals seem to listen to me.

☐ It's really important to me to tell the truth.

☐ I have a great memory.

☐ I have nice handwriting.

☐ I'm a good reader.

☐ I recognize when someone seems to be sad even when she's not real obvious about it.

☐ I tend to see the bright side of things.

☐ I like working on a team.

Ask God to help you see some of the gifts He's put in you. Look over some of the things you've checked in the exercises above. What are the ones that stand out to you as your gifts?

_____

_____

_____

_____

_____

_____

Next, ask your parents or friends to tell you the talents they see in you. Write down some of the things they say.

_____

_____

_____

_____

_____

_____

The truth is, as you try more things, and practice the things you enjoy, you'll learn more and more about all the gifts God's placed in you. The important thing to remember is that *they're in you*. God didn't forget to give you talents or overlook your giftings. They're tucked inside your brain and heart because God has planned for you to do something with them. And He knows exactly what that is.

CHAPTER 3

Once upon a Time

(Making Sense of Your Life Story)

I've had a lot of bad days in my life. I've been fired from Whit's End, had to call off my wedding, and worst of all, received news my mom died.*

Sometimes when I remember the bad stuff or am having a difficult day, it brings up another question we all ask from time to time:

---

* To hear the Adventures in Odyssey audio dramas about these events in Connie Kendall's life, listen to "A Bite of Applesauce" (episode 73, album 5), "Something Blue" (episodes 533–534, album 41), and "Life Expectancy" (episodes 734–736, album 57).

Why doesn't God make my life easier?

You have no idea how many times I've asked myself that question. Why doesn't God just clear the way so we can be happy? I mean, we're on His team, trying to use our gifts to help everybody. Really, we all should have been born with an instruction manual outlining what God wants us to do so we can avoid all the emotional and physical pain. That would make everything so much simpler.

Except my friend Joe has a different take on that idea.

Well, he's not really my friend. He lived a few thousand years ago. And you probably know him better as Joseph. Remember his story? You can read about him in Genesis 37–50.

Joseph's Dream Job

Joseph had a dream job—maybe like your dream to be a professional singer, an Olympic volleyball player, an astronaut, or an artist. But Joseph's dream job was different. His job was to dream when he fell asleep at night. Joseph believed that God gave him the dreams to show him what God wanted for his future.

But those dreams were, ahem, a little hard to swallow: they were about his parents and older brothers bowing down to him. You can probably imagine those dreams didn't go over too well at the dinner table. It's likely he got a few spoonfuls of mashed figs flung his way.

And unfortunately, his brothers didn't stop at a food fight—they went too far in showing Joseph just how much they hated him and his dreams. One day, those brothers were so angry with Joseph, they decided to throw him into a well. To cover up his disappearance, they covered his coat with sheep blood so their father—Jacob—would think a lion had killed Joseph. Then, the brothers sold Joseph as a slave to some travelers who were passing by. (That probably makes your little sister borrowing your hairbrush without asking seem like not such a big deal anymore.)

Can you imagine the conversations Joseph had with God? "God, I thought You wanted me to be honored! But now I'm further from that than ever. I'm a slave in a foreign country! How could this happen? Did You forget about me?"

But although Joseph had every reason to be bitter and angry about this turn of events, he chose to work hard as a slave and have a good attitude. His owner, Potiphar, noticed his work ethic and leadership abilities and put him in charge of the entire household. Things were looking up a bit, but when Potiphar's wife—who had a crush on Joseph—tried to kiss Joseph, he knew that wasn't right and ran away from her. Mrs. Potiphar was pretty angry about that, so she worked up some tears and lied to her husband, accusing Joseph of flirting with *her*. Of course, this infuriated Potiphar, and he had Joseph dragged off to prison.

Forgotten

Poor Joseph. He'd worked diligently, made good choices, behaved righteously, and *still* received punishment. For more than ten years, he sat in the dungeons of Egypt. But once again, his good character was recognized, and the jailor placed him in charge of the other prisoners.

One morning Joseph went to check on a couple of prisoners who were in his charge. They were both disturbed from having dreams they didn't understand. But dreams were Joseph's specialty—remember? his dream job?—and after seeking God's help, he told them both what their dreams meant. Things happened exactly as Joseph predicted. One of these men was the cupbearer to Pharaoh (the ruler of Egypt), and Joseph told the cupbearer he would soon be reinstated as Pharaoh's servant. Three days later, the cupbearer was set free, and Joseph asked him to plead his case before Pharaoh. Joseph hoped justice might finally come, but Genesis 40:23 tells us, "The chief cupbearer, however, did not remember Joseph; he forgot him."

The cupbearer *forgot* Joseph. Just when there seemed to be a tiny glimmer of hope that Joseph might escape prison, he was forgotten. He spent two more difficult years eating stale bread and sleeping on a cold floor.

You Can't Surprise God

Do you notice all Joseph's setbacks? (How can you not?) Brothers who sold him into slavery. A lying woman who sent him to prison. People ignoring him, forgetting him.

You might find yourself in similar situations. Your siblings treat you like rotten fig mush. You do the right thing, yet someone still responds in a hurtful way. You get blamed for something you never did. You get treated unfairly. You ask someone to return a favor, but she moves on and forgets about you. You try so hard but still don't feel like you can get it right.

Joseph's story isn't a happy story—but God used it in amazing ways.

See, if Joseph was going to be a world ruler, God knew he couldn't do it from his family's farm. Joseph needed to get to Egypt and, more specifically, into a place where the pharaoh could hear about him. So even though Joseph must have been confused as to why he ended up in the palace prison, God wasn't the least bit surprised.

Here's a Secret . . .

Sometimes our stories take us to places we don't expect, places we don't want to be. Before I moved to Odyssey, I lived in California. I *loved* it there. I whined and complained and begged my mom not to leave. More than a few times, I made plans to get back on any westbound bus and return to the familiar. But now years later, I realize that God knew exactly what I needed. The friendships I've made here—including meeting Jesus Himself—leave me without a doubt that this is the very best place for me to be.

One day the prison warden told Joseph to go the pharaoh's throne room. The ruler was bewildered by a strange dream he'd had, and no one could tell him what it meant. Except Joseph, because, well, that was the job God gave him. Joseph revealed to Pharaoh that a famine was approaching, and he advised Pharaoh what should be done to save the people from certain death.

This time Joseph wasn't forgotten. Not only did he get the biggest promotion in world history—from prisoner to vice president—but he also saved the people of Egypt and Canaan, where his parents and brothers lived. He saved the brothers who threw him in the pit.

God used even these bad things for good.

Joseph said the same thing when he finally revealed to his brothers that he was the second most powerful person in the land (and when his brothers actually did bow down to him). The brothers intended evil, but "God intended it for good" (Genesis 50:20).

God can use *anything* for good.

Four Lessons from Our Friend Joe

1. *Always remember God has a plan.* Joseph continued to give God glory even when he spent a long time in prison. He might not have known what God was working out, but he still had faith and belief in who God was and that he still mattered to God.

2. *Continue living with character.* If I'd been sold into slavery, I wouldn't care about doing a good job. I'd sweep the dirt under the carpet and put too much lemon in the lemonade, all the while muttering mean things about my brothers back home. But Joseph didn't act this way. He behaved with honor and integrity and worked hard even if he didn't understand why he was there.

3. *Be patient in the waiting.* We often want things to move more quickly than they do. We wonder, *Why can't God hurry up sometimes and fix something, or heal someone, or do a miracle?* I've even prayed to God, *Please just teach me what I'm*

supposed to learn so I can get out of this mess! (FYI: that prayer never works for me.) Just like God knows where He wants you to go, and all the steps along the way, He also knows the timing of it all. If Joseph had been released from prison two years earlier, he wouldn't have been there when Pharaoh needed his dream interpreted. God knows what He's doing.

4. *Learn through your experiences.* Joseph wasn't the most humble boy when he bragged about his dreams, but he learned a lot of humility scrubbing floors and living in a dank prison. He also learned a lot about leadership, serving first as the head of Potiphar's household and later in the prison. He learned to depend on God, to make wise choices, and to care for others. All of these lessons are important for a ruler to know. By the time Joseph was promoted to second most powerful in all the land, he knew how to be a leader that God could use.

God used every one of Joseph's trials to teach him something important. It wasn't just about Joseph biding his time. None of it was pointless. All of it had meaning.

And God does the same thing in your life. Maybe you feel your days are too boring or hard or lonely. But God is using *today* to teach you something about Him and about you. He's also preparing you for what He's called you to do *tomorrow*!

It might be learning diligence while working on a school project you detest. Or learning how to have compassion for others because certain kids are picking on you. Maybe you dread going to piano lessons, but learning how to persevere is the very quality God needs you to have in twenty years.

He is the writer of your story. He knows where it begins, where it ends, and all the obstacles and joys in the middle of it. You're not forgotten, you're not a pawn being moved around in God's giant game of Candy Land. He has a plan.

Why?

Knowing that God has a plan and liking His plan are two different things. You may have questions like these: *How could He let my dad lose his job? Or let my dog die? Or let me be the one everyone makes fun of at school?*

We all have why questions for God. I wondered why my parents got divorced, why people close to me had to die, and why I ended up so hurt in relationships that were really important to me. It would be nice if everything went exactly as we wanted it to—but that doesn't happen on this side of heaven. Someday we'll cross over to the streets of gold in heaven, where pain and loneliness will be distant memories. But right now—today—we live in a world that has "fallen." That means there's evil, sickness, natural disasters, and sin. Lots of it. And as a result, there's spiritual darkness, pain, and struggle.

But that's not where your story ends. It's certainly not where Joseph's story ended. And he wasn't the only one with a surprise ending. The Bible is full of stories about people who were on paths that didn't seem to lead in the right direction but, in the end, led to where God wanted them to be. Why did Moses take the Israelites on a forty-year desert trek that could have been completed in only eleven days? (The delay allowed new leaders to mature and enter the Promised Land at just the right time.) Why did Queen Esther have to marry a husband who had the power to put her to death for interrupting a meeting and who would also allow all her people to be murdered? (She was in the right place at the right time to save the Jews from being wiped out in Persia.) Because God always has a plan even when we don't see it.

Think of it this way: if you were given a couple of puzzle pieces for a thousand-piece puzzle, you would have no idea what the whole puzzle looked like. That confusion is like our lives sometimes. The puzzle pieces don't make sense. But as God starts adding more pieces and fitting them together, we begin to see the bigger picture of our lives. He's connecting our life events piece by piece to make something stunning.

God's stories weren't just written for people three thousand years ago. God wrote them for you. Hebrews 12:2 tells us Jesus is "the author and perfecter of our faith." It's His story from "once upon a time" to "happily ever after." And even though there might be a big, bad wolf or a decade of imprisonment in the middle of it, He's the one writing the pages. And He knows how the story ends.

Take my life, for example. I didn't want my parents to get divorced, I didn't want my mom to have financial difficulties. But these were the things that led to the move to Odyssey.

If I wrote my story, it would look very different. I'd probably have myself sitting on a beach eating gummy bears all day and reading magazines. That sounds nice, but I really don't want that to be the story of my life. I want God's story for me. Because I know He's the best writer in the universe.

Need to be reminded of that? Do what I do! Keep this verse taped to your bathroom mirror so you can see it every day:

"For I know the plans I have for you," declares the LORD, "plans to prosper you and not to harm you, plans to give you hope and a future." (Jeremiah 29:11)

Your Turn

If you mapped out a time line of Joseph's life, you'd see that he had a lot of high and low points. In the space provided, draw a time line based on your life story, with high and low points. The highs might be when you met your best friend, when you became a Christian, or when you became more involved in church. Your lows would be the hard things along the way—maybe the death of a pet, a big disappointment, or the loss of a friend. Pray over your life story, and remember, God uses *all* of it.

CHAPTER 4

Shaved Cats Are Important

(How We Get to Know God)

Penny and I started talking about our friendship the other day when she was making Breakfast Brownies. She calls them that because they have eggs (normal) and bacon (not so normal) in them. But it's also an excuse to have chocolate for breakfast, so I don't complain.

We were remembering how our mutual friend Wooton would tell us about each other. He'd say to her, "Penny, you'd love Connie! She invented the marshmallow-jelly-bean sundae, and she's

41

really funny, and when she gets excited, she talks in this really high voice that makes dogs howl!" And to me, he'd say, "Connie, you've got to meet Penny! She's superartistic, and she can imitate all seven dwarves, and she knitted me a hat out of the lint from my clothes dryer!"

But then I actually met Penny. And I liked her pretty much right away. I loved her quirky sense of humor and how brave she could be.

As we got together for ice cream or long Trivial Pursuit contests, we talked more. And the more Penny and I talked, the more we realized how much we had to talk about! I liked her more as she told me stories of her adventures growing up (she shaved her cat once) and the things that shaped her—like getting lost in an art museum as a kid and spending three hours staring at a painting that's now her favorite. I also appreciated the way she nodded all sympathetically when I talked about things that make me sad, and how she'd awakened me early one morning with a brilliant idea about painting a mural on the living-room wall. And I saw that even when she got fired from her job without good reason, she didn't mope or complain. She just did what she had to do to find a new job. All of these stories and experiences with Penny grew our friendship even deeper.•

---

* To find out more about how Connie met Penny, listen to album 53, *The Green Ring Conspiracy*, episodes 679–690.

Here's a Secret . . .

Sometimes when I take time to pray, I just sit on the couch in my living room, and I imagine Jesus sitting in the chair across from me. (I know God is always with me, but there's something about picturing Him somewhere close by that makes it easier to connect.) Then I talk to Him—just like I would talk to Penny or Wooton or Whit. Sometimes I'll just whisper or mouth the words so anyone walking around doesn't think I'm crazy. But I'll cry with Jesus, and laugh. And as I'm praying/talking, I feel His peace. I can sense Him listening to me. And Bible verses will start coming to mind—or things people have said that I didn't pay much attention to at first, but now . . . well, now they make me think. Even reminders of people I need to forgive or ask forgiveness from will enter my mind, and I'm pretty sure these thoughts are from God. Having these conversations with God always makes me feel closer to Him.

Now, About God . . .

Knowing God is kind of like knowing your best friend. You don't learn who she is by reading a list of her best qualities or seeing a picture of her. You get to know and like her based on your conversations with her and the experiences you share together.

I think that's why the Bible tells a lot of stories. Sure, the Holy Book would be a lot shorter if it just had a few chapters listing God's qualities: creative, all-powerful, loving, disciplining, knows everything, makes lists of rules, compassionate. Some of the things we might like, and some we might not understand or appreciate so much.

I knew *about* Penny.

And then I knew some *stories about* Penny.

And then I *had experiences* with Penny.

And then I *formed a relationship* with Penny to understand her personality.

My journey in coming to know God was just like that (well, except the shaving-the-cat part). There was a time in my life when I had only heard *about* God—people had told me certain qualities or ideas about Him. But when I came to Odyssey, I heard a lot more *stories about* God from the Bible—parables, prophecies, and letters. I heard stories about how God created the earth, had a man swallowed by a fish, and made a donkey talk (yes, really!).* I felt drawn to

---

* These Bible stories can be found in Genesis 1–3, the whole book of Jonah, and Numbers 22:21–39. For the story of Jonah, see also Adventures in Odyssey "Return to the Bible Room" (episode 41, album 2) and "The Final Call" (episode TC8, *The Truth Chronicles*).

this God who is creative and wants what is best for His people. He's powerful and just but also incredibly loving. Then, as I grew more interested, I *had experiences* with God and formed a relationship. I saw Him answer prayers and work things out in ways I never could've imagined. I saw Him change people. I saw Him change me.

And I fell in love with God.

An Invisible God?

Even though I love God, there's no formula for figuring Him out. I'll never understand everything about Him or why He does what He does. I can't manipulate Him to get what I want. He's not a vending machine or a video game. Rules to control Him don't exist. Just like the humans He created, God has a personality. Growing in relationship with Him means learning more about who He is. Getting to know God is similar to growing in my friendships with Eugene, Whit, Penny, and Wooton. The more I got to know them, the more I loved them. Even though Eugene initially drove me crazy with all his statistics and definitions, and Wooton frustrated me by cleaning out our supply of licorice twice a day, now they're some of my favorite people in the world. And then, of course, there was Penny . . . but I already told you about her.

One of my radio listeners asked a great question!

How can I be in a relationship with someone I can't see or hear?

And I have a great answer! You *can* see and hear God. But because He exists in a different realm than we do, we see and hear Him differently than we see and hear our friends, family, or next-door neighbors.

Even though you won't be snapping a selfie with God, you can "see" Him in other ways. Look outside . . . do you see tall trees, skies that change with the weather, or cloud formations? God shows His beauty, power, and majesty in nature. You can see it through the carved rocks of the Grand Canyon to the serene beaches of Tahiti to the tree outside your bedroom window. God made those things—the seasons, the storms, the birds. And you can learn a lot about someone by what he or she makes.

You can also watch God work. The way He answers prayers or works things out when it doesn't seem at all possible. The way someone offers you a word of encouragement when you really need it. Or how you can have the courage to make a good choice and wonder, *Where did that come from?*

And you can hear God. First of all, by reading the Bible. God shows us a lot about Himself through the stories He put in the Bible. The best way to continually grow to know God better is by studying His Word, talking to Him through prayer, watching for what He's up to, and spending time around other people who know Him.

Your Plan to "See" God

1. *Studying the Bible.* To start, select a passage in the Bible. I'd suggest choosing one of the Gospels (Matthew, Mark, Luke, or John) or the Psalms. If it helps, you could even get a devotional book that suggests a passage for you.

    Pray and ask God to clean out your heart. Confess any sin you might have in your life, and ask that your heart would be ready to receive whatever He shows you.

    Read the passage carefully. Jot down the answers to these questions: What does this passage tell me about who God is? Why did God want this passage in the Bible?

    Read the same passage again, slowly. And answer these questions: What does this tell me about my relationship with God? Is there something in my life I need to change, to be more aware of? Are there words of encouragement or promise? Jot some of these down.

Penny's Corner

Okay, Connie asked me if there was anything that the other girls or I wanted to share about how you get to know God. For me, remembering that God created us in His image helps. The things I like about the people around me remind me of the characteristics of God, too. Like Wooton always cracks me up, and then I remember, "Hey, God made Wooton and gave Wooton a great sense of humor. So God must have a really, really great sense of humor too!"

Olivia told us, "I like to journal my prayers. They start out with "Dear Jesus . . ." and then I just write Him. For me, that's easier than talking."

Tamika told us, "Sometimes I hear from God through my pastor or Sunday school teacher. My teacher will give an illustration or talk about a way that we sin, and I realize, "Hey, I do that! God must've put that in the message today for me to hear it."

The way we answer the questions will be different because we're all at different places in life and experiencing different things. But what we do know is that God wants to speak to us. " 'You will seek me and find me when you seek me with all of your heart. I will be found by you,' declares the LORD" (Jeremiah 29:13–14).

Try to avoid skipping around to a bunch of different passages randomly. The Bible is best read in large chunks. That way you can see how the chapters build on each other. If you skip around in the Bible, you won't end up with the best understanding of what's being said. I know a person who used the open-and-point method, where she closed her eyes, opened the Bible, and pointed to a verse. Wherever her finger landed was the verse for the day. (Okay, the person was me.) It didn't work so well, especially when my verse was "Take me a heifer of three years old, and a she goat of three years old, and a ram of three years old, and a turtledove, and a young pigeon."* Uh . . . what was I supposed to do with that?

2. *Prayer.* I think this is one of the most amazing things about God. See, I talk a *lot*. To the point that my friends have to interrupt me and say, "I really have to go!" and run out the

---

* See Genesis 15:9, KJV.

door. But God loves to hear from me. He always wants to know what's on my heart, and He's okay with my rambling. (Talk about a good friend!) He wants to hear from you, too. Even though He already knows you better than you know yourself, He still wants you to tell him how you're feeling.

Sometimes we complicate prayer way too much. We feel like there are special words we should use, or we should be superformal. Like God is sitting across from us at a principal's desk, and we need to be on our best behavior and use correct grammar. Instead, think about God as sitting on the couch across from you or on the step next to you. He doesn't care as much about how elaborate your words are— He cares about your heart! You can talk to Him like you'd talk to a friend.

But remember, prayer is not a list of things we want. I thought at one point that instead of studying for my math test, I would pray that God would give me an A. But my A came in the form of "Aaack! I can't believe I did so bad on this test!" God wants a relationship with you. He isn't your magic genie who gives you whatever you want. God wanted me to actually learn something, not just get a good grade. Go figure.

If you want more ideas on how to pray, you can look at Luke 11. Here the disciples asked Jesus how to pray. (See, even they weren't sure.) Jesus shared a prayer with them that today is known as the Lord's Prayer. Jesus wasn't saying that every time you pray, you should say these exact words; He was giving a model on what prayer could look like. It included worshiping God ("[holy] is your name"), asking for things we want or need ("give us each day our daily bread"), seeking forgiveness ("forgive us our sins"), and requesting help in living a life that pleases Him ("lead us not into temptation"). You can follow the same general format of the prayer, but talk in a way that sounds more like you.

While you pray, don't forget to take a few minutes to simply listen. Sometimes God brings things to mind while we pray. For Tamika's brother, Marvin, he began feeling a nudge that he should give his bike to a boy who didn't have one. It wasn't what he wanted to hear. (He had a really nice bike.) But he knew that's what God wanted him to do, and it was the right thing.*

3. *Pay attention to what's going on around you.* Look around you. What's going on with your church? Is God working in people's lives or in a new ministry that you can be a part of? He might be showing you opportunities around you. Sometimes we grow to know God better through the people He created. He likely placed them around us for a reason. They can speak wisdom and truth into our lives and encourage us.

---

* See "The Nudge" (episode 600, album 47).

Your Turn

Remember what we talked about earlier when we were discussing Bible study? Let's give it a try!

Pick out a Bible passage. If you already read the Bible regularly or you have a daily devotional, just pick up where you left off. If not, try one of your favorite verses, one of the Gospels, or a psalm. Before you read, remember to ask God to prepare your heart for the message He has for you.

Now you're ready to read the passage. What does it tell you about who God is? Why do you think God wanted this passage in the Bible?

_____

_____

_____

_____

_____

_____

Now read the same passage again, slowly and carefully this time. Think about these questions: What does it tell you about your relationship with God? Is there something in your life you feel you need to change or be more aware of? Are there words of encouragement or promise?

_____

_____

_____

_____

_____

_____

If writing down what you learn helps you better understand what God's trying to say to you, grab a notebook or a journal and keep answering these questions every time you read.

CHAPTER 5

We Don't Need Oil Changes

(But We Do Need to Stay Healthy)

When I was sixteen, I bought my first car and named her Melba. I paid for Melba myself—with a little help from my mom. But it quickly became apparent that the responsibility of being a car owner didn't end with the paperwork getting signed. I needed to fill up Melba with gas every week. And do you know cars need their oil changed every three thousand miles? Plus she needed regular tune-ups by the mechanic, snow tires in winter, regular cleaning so she didn't rust out, refills of windshield-wiper fluid, and a whole list of other things. When I did all those things for Melba, she ran well for me. But when I forgot or got lazy about maintenance, I'd end up on the side of the road waiting for someone to come and give me a tow.

The thing is, each one of our bodies is like that. No, we don't need oil changes. But we do need regular maintenance to keep us at our best.

The Bible tells us in 1 Corinthians 6:19–20 that your body is "a temple of the Holy Spirit," and you are to honor God with it. He gave you this one body to use here on earth—so you can run, play, eat, talk, and do a million other things. But your body belongs to God, and that gives us extra incentive to take really good care of it.

To keep yourself running well, remember this memory word: FACES. It stands for

Food

Attitude

Cleanliness

Exercise

Sleep

Let's Start with FOOD

Everything you eat will either make your body healthier or less healthy. When you eat a salad full of vegetables, you'll have energy to concentrate, build stronger muscles and healthier skin, and be less likely to get sick. Eating a package of chocolate-chip cookies, however, increases your risk of disease and causes your organs to work harder than they need to. Even though you might feel energetic after you first eat the cookies, those energy levels will soon decrease, and you'll end up feeling lazy and cranky.

I know, I know . . . I work in an ice-cream shop—sugar central. But I'm not saying you need to give up sweet treats completely; just be aware of how many treats you're eating and be careful that your healthy foods far outnumber the unhealthy ones.

Need more reasons to eat well? Healthy foods help you concentrate better in school, perform better at sports, think more clearly, impact how healthy you'll be as an adult, keep you from becoming overweight, cause your skin to look nicer, and help you sleep better. So even though that donut looks really good, if you think of the cost to your body, maybe you won't eat three.

To get a better idea of your eating patterns, keep track for a day of what you eat—including what you're snacking on between meals.

Breakfast:

_____

_____

_____

Morning snacks:

_____

_____

Lunch:

_____

_____

_____

Afternoon snacks:

_____

_____

Dinner:

_____

_____

_____

_____

Evening snacks:

_____

_____

Here's what you need to do to organize your choices:

1. Circle all the fruits and vegetables.
2. Underline all the whole grains, eggs, dairy, and proteins (meat).
3. Cross out all the foods with sugar, along with any fried foods like chips or french fries.

Ideally, you should have the most circles, then the second-most underlines, and then one or two x's.

Now think of ways you can cut back on the bad foods and increase the better choices. Can you have a piece of fruit after dinner instead of that bowl of ice cream? Or maybe switch out the bag of potato chips at lunch with some crunchy carrot sticks?

We also need to check the ingredients of what we're eating. Having a bowl of cereal might seem like a great idea for breakfast, but look at the first couple ingredients. Are any of them sugar or corn syrup? Again, these are the things that might give you energy for a while, but then they will cause you to crash later. Before you know it, you'll be hungry again. Ask your mom for eggs, whole-wheat toast with peanut butter, yogurt and fruit, or even a cereal with less sugar.

The most important thing is being aware of what we eat. We're often careful about what we look like on the outside—do our shoes match, is our hair combed, is there anything stuck in our teeth? But we give less thought to what we're putting *inside* our bodies. It's like getting a new paint job on my car but not filling it up with gas!

Smile . . . We're Talking About ATTITUDE

A positive look on life can actually add years to your life *and* make the days better.

I'm well aware that it's easier to see the downside of things—I do it all the time. You have to share a room with your sister, and she's totally messy. Your parents give you a crazy amount of chores to do. Your coworker at Whit's End spills ice cream in the freezer, and *you* have to clean it up. There are plenty of things in life to complain about.

Happier people don't necessarily have better lives. They simply choose to have a more cheerful perspective on them. They're more quick to laugh at themselves, recognize the silver lining of situations, and point out all the good things in their lives—even when the bad stuff seems more obvious. Get it? Happiness is more about making a choice to be joyful than it is about having a picture-perfect life.

Here's a Secret . . .

Smiling, even when you force it, actually reduces stress and releases endorphins. (Endorphins are hormones in our brain that make us happy.) So sometimes even making yourself smile will make life a little brighter.

Penny has actually taught me a lot about being joyful. She sees the good in everything. When I burned the toast the other morning, she called it Bread Flambé and spoke with a French accent all during breakfast. And when the car broke down (did I mention how much maintenance those things take?) and we waited an hour for Eugene to come get us, she pointed out the sunset and started a game of I Spy. She makes the most of every moment and appreciates the beauty and good in it. Her enthusiasm is catchy, and my grumbling usually stops when I see how much fun she's having.

It's not easy having a positive perspective on life—especially when we're used to noticing the bad things first. But just like you need practice to learn multiplication tables or perfect that cartwheel, joy takes some practice too.

Having a joyful attitude starts with being aware of what thoughts you're dwelling on. The Bible tells us, "Whatever is true, whatever is noble, whatever is right, whatever is pure, whatever is lovely, whatever is admirable—if anything is excellent or praiseworthy—think about such things" (Philippians 4:8). To give you the shortened version: focus on the good stuff! Your sister might be messy, but she's the best person in the world at keeping a secret. And although emptying the dishwasher every day gets tiring, those dirty dishes mean you ate three good meals that day. And although I'm not a fan of cleaning up spilled ice cream, I *am* grateful that I have a job working at Whit's End.

So when you're feeling discouraged, take a deep breath and re-focus. Are things really as bad as you're making them out to be? Is there something to be grateful for in this moment? Is there something you can do to change a situation instead of simply complain?

Next Up? Keeping It CLEAN

You probably have already heard that as you grow into an adult, a lot of big changes will occur in your body. But there are also some smaller, less noticeable changes. You'll sweat more, and it will probably have a stinkier smell to it. So putting on deodorant might need to be added to your morning routine. Your body starts making more oils, leading to oilier skin. You may notice that your hair is greasier or your skin is breaking out. Getting a few zits isn't the end of the world, but they can be a real bummer on school-picture day. To help, wash your face with a gentle, oil-free cleanser every day. Zits can still crop up, but over-the-counter medications can be pretty effective. And your dermatologist will have other suggestions. As far as your hair goes, you might need to wash it more. But shampooing it too often can cause it to become dry, so figure out what works best for you.

And let's not forget that smile. Since you now have adult teeth, remember these are the teeth you'll have until you're a great-grandparent. (Or until you get false teeth.) So take care of them! Brush twice a day. I usually sing "Rudolph, the Red-Nosed Reindeer" in my head so I know I'm brushing long enough. I tried singing it out loud once, but it just got toothpaste all over my mirror. Remember to floss every day, and for extra cavity-fighting power, swish around some bacteria-fighting mouth rinse.

Good hygiene is about more than not stinking—although, let's face it, that's important. How you take care of your skin and teeth affects the way the rest of your body works. (Did you know people who floss live an average of seven years longer?!) And when we brush out germs from our mouths and wash them off our skin, it keeps us from getting sick.

Most of all, remember that changes are normal as your body grows and develops. You might need to make some adjustments in your routine to accommodate some of these changes, but a healthy body is worth the effort! (Plus, it's nice when people don't avoid you because your armpits stink.)

Ready, Set ... EXERCISE!

Being active has countless benefits for your health. Did you know that kids your age are three times more likely to be obese (very overweight) than kids who grew up thirty years ago? Obesity can cause some pretty serious diseases—like cancer and diabetes. It also greatly limits how well a person performs at sports and school, and being overweight even makes it harder to get a good night's sleep. Obesity is due in a large part to inactivity. Kids like to stay inside and watch TV or play electronic games instead of riding their bikes or playing games at the park. But in the long run, exercise makes you feel a whole lot better than a half hour of television. Remember those feel-good endorphins we talked about earlier? Exercise causes them to release in our brains, creating feelings of happiness and reducing stress.

But the benefits of exercise don't end there. Another great reason to be active now is because it will build strong bones for later in life. We've all seen little old ladies hunched over because as they've aged, their bones have deteriorated. I know that seems like forever away, but the reality is that the *only* time in your life you can increase your bone strength is from childhood until age twenty-five. After that, there's nothing you can do. So even though looking ahead fifty years is hard to do when you're more concerned about zits than wrinkles, the "grandma" you in the future will thank the "exercising" you now.

So, as a reminder, here's how being active can help you:

1. It makes you better at sports.
2. It gives you more energy, allowing you to do more things.
3. It puts you in a better mood.
4. It helps you sleep better.
5. It prevents diseases both now and in the future.
6. It increases your bone strength.

Penny's Corner

I like to bike or run with a friend—well, whenever Connie remembers to show up! For me, things are always more fun when you do it with someone you enjoy. And laughing strengthens your stomach muscles. (I have very strong stomach muscles.)

I asked the other girls what they do to keep in shape. Here's what they said.

Camilla told me, "Everything! I'm involved in soccer, volley-ball, and basketball, and I love team sports of all kinds. I don't even think about how tired I am because I'm having so much fun with my friends! I also have a contest with my sister every night to see who can do the most push-ups!"

Olivia said, "I suggest ways that we can be more active as a family. Instead of watching a movie together, we could go roller skating. Instead of going out to eat, we could take a hike with a picnic lunch. Other ideas are biking, playing soccer in the backyard, swimming, or taking a walk around the neighborhood. Once we even created our own exercise circuit around the backyard. We had to jump on the trampoline, swing on the swings, jump-rope, do sit-ups, and climb a tree. We finished off with a water-balloon fight to cool ourselves off. We had fun as a family and got a great workout!"

Tamika's advice is this: "I walk home from school instead of having my mom pick me up. I like having the time to think about my day and clear my head before I need to start my homework."

And here's Emily's take: "I found an activity I really enjoy: tae kwon do. So I try to go to classes whenever I can. I'm not that great at it, but it's fun, and that's what matters. I have other friends who enjoy skateboarding, ballet, or gymnastics. The key is trying a few different activities and finding something you love."

Stay Awake for This Part . . . SLEEP

When I first started junior high school, I didn't get tired as early in the evening. So, of course, I stayed up later—playing games on my computer, texting my friends, and listening to music. Eventually I'd shut my eyes for a snooze. But even though I could choose what time I fell asleep, I couldn't choose the time I had to wake up for school. At 6:00 a.m. my alarm would rudely beep me into consciousness, and . . . well, I'd throw it across the room. Ten minutes later, my mom would come shake me awake. "Connie, Connie!" she'd say, almost shouting. "You need to get up! You'll be late for school!" I'd crawl deeper under my comforter. She'd resort to singing loudly, tickling, or even sliding ice cubes down the back of my pajamas in order to wake me. Needless to say, it wasn't very fun for either of us.

I'd shuffle through my morning and doze off in study hall that afternoon, but by the time evening rolled around again, I'd be wide awake. So the cycle continued.

What I've learned since then is that as we enter the teen years, our biological clock (also called our *circadian system*) shifts. We start feeling tired later. But—and here's the key—that doesn't mean we should go to bed later.

And besides the torture of getting out of bed in the morning, is sleep really that important?

In a word . . . yes! One study showed that kids who got one

hour less of sleep per night than their classmates performed two grade years below in their schoolwork. That means a sixth grader was doing the same level of work as a fourth grader, and it was simply because she went to bed one hour later!

Here's a Secret . . .

Just like developing any new skill takes time, forming healthy habits doesn't happen overnight. Even if they're bad for us, old habits tend to stay with us because our brains have become so used to them. It takes a lot of time practicing healthy routines for them to become habits. Luckily, it doesn't take too long to retrain ourselves—maybe just a couple of months. Before long, these healthy habits become so much a part of our lives that we hardly have to think about them anymore. That's what it really means to have a healthy lifestyle.

Another study showed that the more sleep we get, the more the things we've learned during the day become ingrained into our brains. We might think staying up late to study will help us do better on a test the next day. But the truth is, we're better off getting more sleep so what we did study can seep deeper into our memories and allow us to recall it when test time comes.

And let's not forget how cranky I was on those days I wasn't getting enough sleep. I'm sure Whit remembers the time I burst into tears because we ran out of chocolate sprinkles. (That's tragic and all, but not tear worthy.) A typical teen girl already has emotional mood swings due to hormones, and a lack of sleep can make emotions even more out of control.

One radio listener complained . . .

Q: But I feel like such a baby going to sleep early!

Maybe you'd feel better if you knew the genius Albert Einstein slept ten hours a night, even as an adult. And that the great inventor Thomas Edison took naps every day. The US Olympic Committee encourages their athletes to get nine or ten hours of sleep each night for peak performance.

You're not a little kid anymore, but you're still growing, and that requires a *lot* of energy. So even though it might seem like going to bed earlier is a childish thing to do, it really is an important part of taking care of yourself.

You may feel like Olivia, who asked this question:

> **Q.** But even when I go to bed early, I have trouble falling asleep. What do I do?

If you have trouble falling asleep, here are some things that may help.

1. *Avoid eating a couple hours before you go to bed, especially sugars.* After you swallow your food, a little party happens. Your stomach, intestines, liver, gallbladder, and pancreas (the digestive tract) break down food. This series of biochemical festivities can keep the rest of your body awake. And sugars will give you a quick jolt of energy, making you too antsy to get good rest.

2. *Lights out. Total darkness is best for sleep.* It's even a good idea to turn your clock radio around. When we can't sleep, we often will keep looking at the clock. And then we get stressed out because it's taking us so long to fall asleep, making it even harder to do so!

3. *Think good thoughts.* Avoid replaying the moment you tripped over Kenny Phillips's desk and knocked your teacher into a potted plant. Now is the time to focus on good memories or dreams you have for yourself. I'll sometimes try to think of a hundred things to thank God for—waffles for breakfast, a compliment from Penny, the ability to read, friends who love me, the beauty of stars, sunshine—and usually by the time I get to number thirty-four, I'm asleep.

4. *Drink milk.* Grandma was right: a warm glass of milk before bed helps you sleep. And it doesn't even have to be warm, because milk has a lot of protein. A quick dose of protein before bedtime helps your body fall asleep faster. (But not too big and not too close to bedtime—see point 1 in this list.)

5. *Do something relaxing before bed.* Try taking a bath or reading a good book. If your brain is already in a restful state, your body will follow suit sooner. But, take note, the flickering lights of a TV actually activate your brain; the lights don't relax it. So watching a favorite show right before bed might make it *more* difficult to fall asleep.

You've been blessed with an amazing body that can do amazing things! So take better care of it than I did with Melba. I could sell her after a few years, but that "temple" (remember 1 Corinthians 6:19–20?) of yours has to last a lifetime!

Your Turn

Let's find out where you are with FACES. Take this short quiz by checking the box that best matches your lifestyle. (Be honest! If you've been thinking green-apple-flavored Jolly Ranchers are a fruit, you need to adjust your eating habits! Or if you think cleanliness is merely changing underwear every day, you need to start with a brain wash!)

1. FOOD: When I need a snack, I usually reach for . . .
   - ☐ potato chips or a candy bar
   - ☐ pretzels or popcorn
   - ☐ carrots or celery sticks (with peanut butter, of course)

2. ATTITUDE: When faced with an unexpected challenge, I usually say . . .
   - ☐ "Gah! *Another* thing on my plate!"
   - ☐ "Okay, let's work through this."
   - ☐ "Bring it on!"

3. CLEANLINESS: I wash my face _____ time(s) a day.
   - ☐ 0
   - ☐ 1
   - ☐ 2 or more

4. EXERCISE: I get at least thirty minutes of physical activity
    _____ time(s) a week.
    ☐ 0–2
    ☐ 2–4
    ☐ 4 or more

5. SLEEP: I usually sleep _____ hours a night.
    ☐ 4–6
    ☐ 6–7
    ☐ 8 or more

Now look back over your answers. In which areas did you mark the first box? For each of those, think of a new habit you can start today. If you checked any middle boxes, consider how you can make a change that will move you toward the third box. Write your ideas below.

_____

_____

_____

_____

_____

CHAPTER 6

Even Car Crashes Get Attention

(Clothes, Trends, and a Little Thing Called Modesty)

Once upon a time, the queen told her people that her new favorite food was eggs. So the entire kingdom, wanting to be like their beloved queen, went to the store and bought eggs. They fried them for breakfast, boiled them for lunch, and scrambled them for dinner. Just as they were growing accustomed to eating eggs all the time, the queen made another announcement.

"Eggs are no good, and I shall never eat another one," the

beloved queen shouted from the castle terrace. "But asparagus is wonderful, and I shall heretofore eat it at every meal!"

Once again the people of the kingdom followed suit. That very day the people dumped dozens of eggs into the garbage, and farmers planted asparagus in all their fields. Asparagus soufflés cooled on windowsills, children snacked on asparagus sandwiches in the schoolyard, and the local restaurant added asparagus Jell-O to its dessert menu. But six months later, asparagus was piling up in the markets and rotting, all because the queen had decided she now liked . . . cheddar cheese.

It's ridiculous, isn't it? An entire kingdom basing what they enjoyed, bought, and used because one person decided that's what *she* liked? And what she liked kept changing!

The truth is this happens every day in our country, and all around the world. But it's not what we eat—it's what we wear!

Get Off the Trend-mill

For young women, there can be a lot of pressure on how we look and dress. Americans spend eighty-two million dollars each year to stock their closets. The fashion industry dictates what looks good and what doesn't. The industry tells you what you should be wearing and what you should throw away.

Every year there are fashion trends—items that become must-have articles of clothing. But, just as quickly, these same sweaters and scarves become unpopular. And crowds of people need to go back to the store to buy the next thing they're supposed to have.

Yep . . . sounds about as ridiculous as ordering asparagus Jell-O at your favorite restaurant. Yet we're willing to pay a crazy amount of money for a pair of jeans, simply because of the label on the back pocket. Or wear painful shoes that make us miserable just because they're the "in" thing.

I once bought a jacket with all these sparkly beads on it because the saleslady told me it was the "new hot thing," and all my friends would be talking about it. And she was right. As soon as I set foot in Whit's End, Eugene took one look at the shiny jacket and said, "Cease and desist! Kindly remove that abhorrently blinding object!" Then he put on his sunglasses because the jacket's glare was so bright, he couldn't look straight at me. I returned the jacket the next day.

I'm not telling you to dismiss how you look and wear a paper bag to school tomorrow. (Please, *please*, don't do that.) There's nothing wrong with looking nice or buying cute clothes.

Adorn Your Temple

In chapter 5 we talked about how our bodies are temples of the Holy Spirit, and how it's our responsibility to take care of them. It's also our responsibility to keep them looking nice. Even God cares about appearance, especially about the place where He was worshiped in Old Testament days. (You guessed it—the temple.)

When God's temple was being built, Solomon designed it this way: "On the walls all around the temple, in both the inner and outer rooms, he carved cherubim, palm trees and open flowers. He also covered the floors of both the inner and outer rooms of the temple with gold" (1 Kings 6:29–30).

Gems, fine linens, elaborate carvings, floors of gold?! This temple wasn't shabby—it was gorgeous, the most beautiful building in its day. Why would God care what His building looked like? I think it's because of what the outward appearance of the temple said about the inside. When the people looked at this awe-inspiring building, they were reminded it represented an awe-inspiring God who happened to live inside!* A God who was holy, perfect, glorious, and worthy of worship.

So what does the *outside* of you communicate about the *inside* of you? (Circle all that apply.)

- I like a certain sports team.
- I'm gentle and sweet.
- I don't care how I look.
- I'm sporty.
- I'm fun.

---

* God's presence dwelled on top of the ark of the covenant, which was parked inside Solomon's temple. See the spine-tingly, mysterious details in Leviticus 16:2; 1 Kings 6:19; 8:6–11; and 2 Chronicles 5:13–14.

- I'm unique.
- I shop at a certain store.
- I go to a certain school.
- I'm bold and vivacious.
- I'm feminine.
- I'm laid-back.
- I follow the crowd and wear what they wear.
- I'm particular and fussy.
- I create my own trends.
- I need attention.

You don't need to plate yourself in gold, but the way you dress does communicate how you see yourself. Penny has a great story about this.

Penny's Corner

In high school, I was in a play where I was cast as a snooty old lady. My character wore these outrageous fur coats and large, gaudy pieces of jewelry. When it was time for costuming, I was able to find a coat at a thrift store, but there wasn't any cheap jewelry available.

After mentioning my dilemma to my mom, she had an idea. We went to the basement where she proceeded to sort through a pile of cardboard boxes.

As she dug inside a box, she explained. "When your great-aunt Eunice passed away, your grandmother gave me a couple boxes of her things. These were boxes Eunice kept in the basement. She loved cheap trinkets and gaudy jewelry. I couldn't bear to throw them away, since they're all I have to remember her by, but I never use any of it. Aha! Here it is!" She handed me a dusty cardboard box brimming with, well, junk.

I fumbled through moldy snow globes, cheap earrings that fell apart at a touch, and fat, pink plastic bracelets. But then I saw it: a sticky, tarnished chain with a large, green glass stone dangling from it. "This is perfect," I told her. "The audience will be able to see this thing from the back row!"

The next day I passed it around to the rest of the cast. They all agreed it was perfect.

After our final bow on opening night, an elderly man approached me.

"Excuse me, miss," he said. "Do you mind if I take a closer look at that necklace?"

I handed it over to him, curious why anyone would be interested in an old piece of jewelry.

Much to my surprise, he pulled out a little, round jeweler's eyepiece. He used it to examine the necklace up close.

"I'm an antique dealer," he explained after a few minutes. "And I believe this might be a rare emerald necklace from the Victorian era."

I must've been staring at him in utter shock, because he added, "Truly. It's likely very valuable."

Sure enough, after a complete appraisal of the stone, we learned the necklace we found in Great-Aunt Eunice's dusty junk box was worth nearly ten thousand dollars! What I'd thought was green glass was actually a very large emerald, but it was just too dirty to be recognized. Once it was cleaned up, the piece was absolutely stunning! I thought back to how it had been stored in a damp basement for years with a bunch of junk, how I'd tossed it so carelessly into my backpack and thrown it around to my friends for them to see. Now my mom keeps it in a velvet-lined case and displays it in our front room. Every month she unlocks the glass cover to polish the emerald with an expensive cleaning solution. Yep, that necklace deserved a way better spot than a box in the basement!

Here's a Secret . . .

Fashion ads will try to tell you exactly what you have to wear. But no matter how trendy a style might be, it won't look good if it doesn't fit you. Everyone has a different body type. Some girls have long legs. Other girls have curves. The trick to having great style is finding clothes that flatter you. That means tight isn't always right. Clothes that are too small will cling to you and make you look uncomfortable. Clothes that are too big will make you look sloppy. The first step to fabulous fashion is buying clothes that fit, even if you have to go up a size.

Penny's story reminds me that others will take cues on who we are by how we portray ourselves. When we dress in clothing that is revealing and tasteless, we communicate that we don't have a lot of self-respect. Essentially, it's saying, "I don't think I'm worth that much." Everyone assumed that Great-Aunt Eunice's necklace was worthless because it was "dressed" so shabbily. Stuck in a box of junk in the basement, no one expected it to be so precious. When we dress our hearts and souls in trashy clothes, we're not giving ourselves credit for how valuable we are. But when we dress modestly and tastefully, it shows that we respect and honor our bodies. That we value what's inside. Similarly, when people walk into Penny's mom's house, they'll notice the necklace in the lovely display and immediately think, *This must be something of value. I want to know more about it!* Dressing modestly shows that we believe we're worth more than being gawked at—that what's *inside* the skin is priceless.

Attention Getters

Recently a caller asked me this question:

Q: My friends wear clothes that my parents won't let me wear. And it seems like they get a lot of attention for it. Why is it so bad?

It's true that girls who dress immodestly might get more attention. Guys might call out to them or whistle at them. But is that really the kind of attention you want? Attention is not the same as admiration. Even car crashes get attention.

Think about Penny's emerald necklace. Without recognizing how valuable it was, people treated the necklace carelessly and without respect. People who give attention to you only for wearing immodest clothing will quickly set their eyes on the next girl who's wearing a tight skirt. That kind of attention doesn't last. The opinions that matter are from the people who really *know* you—your heart, interests, and opinions—not just those who raise their eyebrows when you walk by.

The Person you should be trying to please the most already admires you. Read the following verses:

> He will exult over you with joy, He will be quiet in His love, He will rejoice over you with shouts of joy. (Zephaniah 3:17, NASB)

> You have stolen my heart with one glance of your eyes. (Song of Songs 4:9)

> He has brought you into his own presence, and you are holy and blameless as you stand before him without a single fault. (Colossians 1:22, NLT)

Read those verses again. Really, right now. *This* is how God sees you. You are lovely and pure, delightful, His bride. Why do we settle for being seen as any less than that? Why do we want attention for a designer pair of jeans or heavy makeup when we have the attention of a God who thinks we're absolutely stunning?

When you go shopping or get dressed in the morning, remind yourself who you are and how God sees you. Dress your temple in a way that communicates that beauty. Feel free to wear that pretty gold necklace or new top that's supercute. God created beauty. He thinks you're beautiful, and He's given you beautiful things to enjoy. But part of the beauty is the mystery—the unknown. Draw others in to notice the important things about you: your heart, your brain, your personality, and the God who dwells in your temple.

Your Turn

We girls always have and always will love clothes. When it isn't an obsession or a modesty issue, putting together an outfit can be an awesome way to bring out your creativity. So let's talk fun fashion!

What's your most positive feature? What's the one thing that you'd want someone to know about you at first glance? Are you . . .

- ❏ bright and happy?
- ❏ fun and charismatic?
- ❏ energetic and athletic?
- ❏ creative and artistic?
- ❏ gentle and kind?
- ❏ classy and calm?
- ❏ smart and confident?
- ❏ a Jesus-girl through and through?

Draw some creative combinations that will reflect the fact that you can set your own trend and that you're a beloved daughter of God.

CHAPTER 7

No, You're Not Crazy

(Managing Your Emotions)

When I broke up with my fiancé, Mitch, I got into a bit of a funk. Well, more than a bit. Even though I knew ending our relationship was the right thing to do, I still missed him a lot. I really thought we would get married, and so letting go of that dream—along with the friendship we had—was painful.* I started watching a lot of TV.

---

* Listen to "Something Blue, Parts 1 and 2" (episodes 533–534, album 41) for the whole sad story.

See, everything reminded me of Mitch—a bowling ball, the color green (Mitch had amazing green eyes), a computer, a restaurant where we had dinner, Whit's End where we hung out. Well . . . I could go on for about nine pages with things that reminded me of him. But each time I felt that sadness, I'd go home and watch TV. It was my way of trying to forget the hurt, to escape the pain. But it quickly became a habit. I watched movies while I ate dinner, and the late, late show until the early morning hours, so I wasn't getting much sleep either. I convinced myself that if I was watching someone else's life, I didn't have to think about mine.

Here's a Secret . . .

Girls, studies show that a lot of people, nearly 10 percent, will suffer from a really deep depression at some point in their lives. And girls are at greater risk than boys. That's the bad news. The good news is that your doctor can do a lot to help you. So if you're really sad or thinking about hurting yourself, talk to your parents, a school nurse, or your doctor. God has put adults into your life to help you—you're not alone.

But that didn't help me get over Mitch. It was like sweeping crumbs under a rug. (Not that I *ever* do that.) The problem was still there. I just wasn't dealing with it. It wasn't until Wooton, Whit, and my mom called me on it. I had to talk things out. I had to let myself be sad. I had to think about it—that's the only way to really heal and move on. I also needed to be around upbeat people and do some fun things so I wouldn't just wallow in self-pity. And watching TV does not count as hanging out with friends.

So when a caller asked this question . . .

Q: I'm a generally happy person with a pretty good life. But lately there are days when I'm depressed for no reason. What's wrong with me?

. . . I felt like I could give a pretty good answer. But just in case, I asked some friends if they knew what this girl was talking about. Oh, boy, did they . . .

> OLIVIA: I was leaving school and slipped on the sidewalk and fell down. It hurt, but not that much. Looking back, it honestly wasn't that big of a deal. But at the time, I burst into tears. I didn't even know why I reacted so strongly.

TAMIKA: I feel like every day is either the best day ever or the worst day ever—there aren't many days in the middle. Some days, everything goes my way, and I have the best friends and family and school and everything. And then the next day—even though I have the same friends, family, and school—I feel like my life is the worst ever. Some days I feel like I'm pretty and good at things. Other days I feel like the ugliest girl in my class and good at absolutely nothing. I don't understand it.

EMILY: My brother gets on my nerves. A lot. And usually I simply leave the room when he's being superannoying. But the other day he kept asking if he could test out his superglue by gluing me to the washing machine. Of course, I said no. And usually that would be the end of it, but instead I got really mad at him. I told him he was the worst brother ever and that I wished he was out of my life!

I don't know why I reacted as strongly as I did. He's been way more annoying other times—trust me!

Maybe you've had sudden bursts of emotion that you couldn't fully explain. If you have, don't worry! You're not crazy. Every girl experiences moments like that—when it feels like emotions are going wacko. But the truth is, it's all a normal part of growing up.

We know that we're changing on the outside. We're expecting to grow taller and heavier and that our bodies will change shape. But what's harder to understand are all the changes that are taking place *inside*. We can't measure with a ruler or scale the ways our brains are changing, moving, and growing. But here's an interesting fact: your brain goes through more changes in early adolescence than at any other time in your life, except when you're a baby.

But just like a changing body causes growing pains, your brain has pains of its own. Different areas of the brain are growing at different rates and are not necessarily communicating well with each other yet. Additionally, a number of chemicals—known as hormones—are being released. As you grow older, the hormones even out, and you feel more normal. But there will be stages during your teen years when they'll be out of balance, and your emotions will be very intense or just all over the place.

Olivia once asked me,

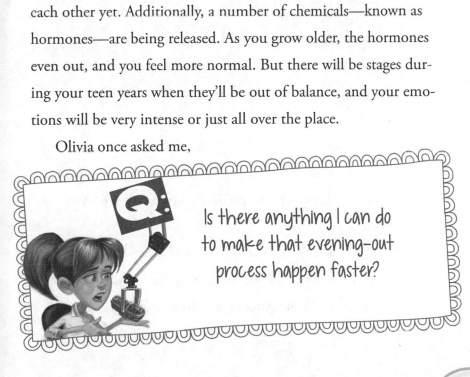

Is there anything I can do to make that evening-out process happen faster?

Sorry . . . I wish I could say spin around in a circle and eat a chocolate sundae and you'll be fine, but there's no "cure" or easy way to even out your emotions. You just have to wait it out. But there are a few things that can help . . .

1. *Remind yourself it's all temporary.* You might feel like you're worthless, that no one likes you, that life is meaningless, that you're dumb, or that everyone's laughing at you. In those moments, remind yourself it's just your brain playing tricks on you. It *seems* like that, but it's not really true.

2. *Your feelings are important.* If self-talk doesn't help or you can't snap your fingers and change the emotions welling up inside of you, cry if you need to. Hit a pillow if you're angry. Talk to your mom if you're feeling confused and don't know what to think about something. But don't feel like you need to bottle up your emotions. Think of your emotions as warning lights on my car, Melba. Her dashboard lets me know when she's overheating or needs oil. So when your emotional dashboard is blinking, stop to find out what the problem is.

3. *Remember that you are totally normal.* Everyone from Albert Einstein to Taylor Swift experienced adolescent mood swings. Your parents, teachers, and even your pastor all went through this. And you've probably already re-

alized your classmates have similar ups and downs—even the kids who seem like they have nothing to be "down" about. Billions of people have traveled this path and survived.

Getting Help

Visiting a counselor or psychologist can be extremely helpful. And although you might feel a little nervous about talking to a stranger about personal stuff, it's nothing to feel embarrassed or worried about. We all need help talking through our problems sometimes or even getting to the root of what is bothering us in the first place. And that's what counselors love to do. There are some ways you can alleviate the bummed-out feelings.

1. *Run away from them.* Seriously, go for a run. Or jump on a trampoline, or do a hundred jumping jacks. When we exercise, chemicals called endorphins are released in our brains. These are also called "feel good" chemicals. They elevate our mood.

2. *Write it out.* Journaling is my favorite way of cheering myself up—especially since I'm not a big fan of exercise. Often we're feeling a lot of emotions and the pressure builds and builds—like air in a balloon—until we feel like we might explode. But when we write out how we

feel, it's like releasing some air out of the balloon. Life seems more manageable, and the simple action of naming my emotions makes them feel less overwhelming. Another way to release the emotion is to sit down for a heart-to-heart talk with your mom or call a friend and tell her about your bad day.

3. *Eat "happy" foods.* We talked about eating well in chapter 5. And with your hormone levels trying to even themselves out, good nutrition is more important than ever. As much as you might feel like eating a big bowl of ice cream or drinking a soda when you're feeling discouraged, that will likely have the opposite effect of what you want. Sugar will cause an energy spike, and then you'll crash lower than you were before. So even though it might be nice to have a treat, an hour later you could be feeling worse than ever. Instead, reach for foods that are high in omega-3 fatty acids. This handy nutrient helps the mood centers of our brains function well. You can fill up on omega-3s by eating nuts and fish. (But make sure you're not allergic! Penny's face swelled up when she ate salmon in an effort to get happier!)*

---

* For the whole story, listen to "Happy Hunting" (episode 720, album 56).

NO, YOU'RE NOT CRAZY

Vitamin B and folate, which are found in brown rice, avocados, fish, and veggies, can also put a positive boost on our emotions. Some studies suggest that females who suffer from depression aren't getting enough folate. So adding some extra folate-rich foods to your diet is a great idea. And don't forget to drink plenty of water. We might not recognize when our bodies are becoming dehydrated, but that causes energy to lag, and our emotions won't be far behind.

4. *Go outside.* Take a walk. Read in the backyard. Not only does fresh air naturally makes us feel energized, but sunshine is also a primary source of vitamin D. This vitamin is necessary for producing serotonin—our built-in mood regulator. That's why some people get more depressed during the winter months when there's not as much sunlight—or vitamin D. If it's cloudy or cold out, you can get vitamin D from milk or by taking a supplement.

5. *Try some tunes.* Energetic music can lift your mood and make you want to dance. Relaxing music can calm you down. (Some hospitals use music to relax patients before surgery.) Try a variety of your favorite songs to see what works best for you.

Penny's Corner

What cheers me up is hanging out with friends. Connie always makes me laugh, and that lifts my mood. One time she put on this wild wig and bright lipstick and sang show tunes. She didn't know that Wooton and Eugene were watching from the porch. When they knocked, she tried to hide inside the Tupperware cabinet. I laughed so hard I cried—but happy tears. Something about being social lifts me out of the doldrums. Usually I'm like, "No . . . I don't want to do that. I feel terrible." But if I actually make the effort to go to the movies or hang out at the park with some friends, I almost always feel better.

Tamika told me that she offers to help someone with something when she's blue. "Whether it's making dinner with my mom or raking leaves for the elderly lady next door, there's something about being helpful that gets my mind off my problems. When I start thinking about others, I often forget what was bothering me in the first place. Sometimes I'll even pray for the little boy we sponsor in Rwanda and remind myself I have a whole *lot* to be thankful for compared to so many others in the world."

Olivia says, "Sometimes I just need a good cry. I'll even put on sad music or a tearjerker of a movie, and just let myself cry. Afterward, I feel lighter and kind of relieved."

For Emily, taking a hot bath and getting lost in a good book are key to a good mood. "I find that pampering myself relaxes me."

Oh, I just remembered one more very important tip! It always helps me to remind myself of God's promises of hope in the Bible. I like reading the Psalms—talk about mood swings! The psalmist goes from wanting to chop off people's heads to singing about how great everything is. I love how even in Bible times, people would feel sad and discouraged, but joy was always right around the corner. And it is for me, too.

You might need to test out a few things and figure out what's helpful for you. Everyone's different. And if you think of something else, let me know!

Your Turn

Have you had any recent moments when your emotions felt uncontrollable? Jot one down if you remember it:

_____

_____

_____

Are you having what Penny calls "the doldrums" right now? Look up the following verses. Does God care about how you're feeling?

- Deuteronomy 31:8

    Hint: God promises never to leave you.

- Psalm 3:3

    Hint: God wants to protect and comfort you.

- Psalm 34:17

    Hint: God knows when you're sad.

- Psalm 42:11

    Hint: God's salvation can give you hope.

- John 16:33

    Hint: God is bigger than any problem you'll face.

CHAPTER 8

When Mom And Dad Spells MAD

(How to Get Along with Parents)

You don't understand me!" I screamed. "You don't even care about me!"

I stormed out of the house, slamming the door behind me. My heart raced, and tears streamed down my cheeks. *How could they do this to me?*

I ran down the sidewalk to the park and climbed to the tip-top of the swing set. It's where I always went when I was upset with Mom and Dad—and it seemed like I'd been there an awful lot lately.

I wiped the tears off my face. Brittany had asked me to go to a party. Brittany—the most popular girl at school! And just because my grandma was visiting, my parents weren't letting me go. It was only one night! Brittany would never ask me again if I turned down her invite. My parents didn't even care that they were officially ruining my entire social life for the next six years by not allowing me to go.

Perfect Parents?

This wasn't the first argument I'd had with my parents, nor—unfortunately—would it be the last. Arguments about friends, chores, clothes, money, social activities, my room, curfews, grades, and a million other things popped up on a daily basis.

Eventually we fought about their divorce. And then my mom and I fought again about her decision to move to Odyssey.

I used to think my parents knew everything. My mom could tie shoes and help me with impossible multiplication problems. My dad could make delicious grilled-cheese sandwiches and ride a motorcycle. Whenever I had a question, they always knew the answer.

But then I think my questions got harder. And they remembered less and less of what it's like to be a kid.

It's pretty common to clash with your parents during your preteen and teen years. You're growing in your independence and wanting to do more on your own or with friends. Your parents want to protect you from getting hurt or into trouble. It's like a game of tug-of-war. You pull on your side of the rope, they pull on theirs, and it doesn't seem like any progress is made—except that you're all getting tired!

But even with the disagreements, you and your parents can enjoy each other during this stage. Read on to find out what Penny and the girls have learned . . .

Penny's Corner

I learned that my parents were concerned that they were losing their little girl. I was changing. I liked my friends and sometimes chose hanging out with them over spending time with my parents. (Mostly because my parents were going to be sitting around, and my friends were going out and doing things I thought were more fun.) But I realized my folks really just wanted to stay connected with me. So I made sure I was home for dinner every night and set up times for my dad and me to go kayaking together—something we both enjoyed doing.

Olivia: I asked my parents about what it was like for them when they were my age. They got into the question a little too much—pulling out photo albums and memorabilia from their high school. It was really funny seeing my dad's yearbook photo (his hair was crazy!) and hearing about my mom's swim-team competitions (she was the only swimmer who used a life jacket). It helped me understand that they used to be tweens and teens too. They knew what it was like—at least a little. And it also reminded them what it's like to be my age and to want to grow up.

Tamika: I invited my parents into my life more—introducing them to my friends, making sure they knew when all my softball games were, telling them about the funny things that happened in English class. They were really interested, and I think it helped them realize that I really am doing okay.

Did you notice that all these suggestions involve communication? That's really key for this time of life. Especially when you disagree with your parents about something.

Donna Drama

My friend Donna—who's now in college—once complained to me about her parents not extending her curfew for the homecoming football game. "Everyone is going out for pizza afterward, and it will be so much fun! I can't believe Mom and Dad want me home by nine thirty! Most of my friends will be hanging out until at least midnight!"

"What did you do to try to change their minds?" I asked her.

Donna gave me a wide-eyed look. "How did you respond to them?" I clarified.

"Well, I whined and complained. And told them all the kids were doing it, and they weren't being fair. And then I kicked a chair and left."

I smiled. Yep, she sounded just like me.

Donna babbled on. "Clearly, I'm mature enough to make my own decisions! I don't know why they can't see that!"

"Maybe because you're demonstrating it to them by throwing a temper tantrum, complete with kicking and complaining."

"Oh." She looked up at me sheepishly. "What should I have done?"

"Make your case. Very calmly, at a convenient time—"

"So not when Dad first walks in the door and Mom is stressed about burning dinner?"

"Right." I thought back to my own conversations with my parents. "When everyone is relaxed and calm, explain your side. What you want, why you want it, and why you think you deserve it."

Donna's head bobbed. "That's easy enough."

"Sure, but this is the hard part." I leaned in closer. "You have to *listen* to them. If they have concerns, ask them what they are and really hear them out. Don't just argue over them."

Donna bit her lip. "I *think* I can do that."

I remembered one more thing. "Oh, and Donna, whatever their response, handle it maturely. Thank them for listening to you. Because down the road, you'll ask for something else, and they'll remember your response to this."

The next day, she stopped by Whit's End again.

"So . . . how'd it go?" I asked as soon as she sat down.

"Pretty good. They said they appreciated my mature attitude . . ."

"And . . ."

"And that they might consider it *next* time."

"Oh. I'm sorry, Donna."

"Yeah, I'm pretty disappointed. But I took your advice and asked them why—not the whining why-y-y-y-y? but the I-really-want-to-understand-why why."

I was so proud of her. "Good for you! What did they say?"

"First, that last time a bunch of kids went out after the game, several of them ended up getting in trouble with the police for vandalizing a restaurant. It wasn't my friends that did it, but I kind of understood their concern. The other thing they said was even harder to hear . . ."

"What was that?"

"That the last time I said I'd be home by ten, I was late. And they were worried." She looked down at her shoes. "So they said they can't trust me."

"Ouch."

Here's a Secret . . .

It always helps to vent about things that irritate you. But remember that your parents have your best interests at heart. If you're feeling angry at your parents, write down your frustrations before trying to talk to them about it. Write a list of things you love about your parents before you try discussing a disagreement. While planning out your discussion strategy, remember that your relationship with your parents matters most. Getting the anger out before you talk and keeping love in mind while you talk will help keep discussions from turning into heated arguments.

Donna took a deep breath. "I know. I apologized to them for being late, and my mom had a good suggestion. She said maybe I could invite a few of my friends over after the game, and we could have pizza at our house instead."

"That sounds like a great idea."

I saw a glimmer in Donna's eyes as she responded. "I thought so too. I mean, it would still be fun to go out, but if I can show my parents I can be responsible and keep my word, I think next time they just might let me stay out later."

She was right. A month later Donna's parents extended her curfew to eleven o'clock. And this time she didn't break it.

Parents Aren't Perfect … Neither Are We

Yes, your parents will make mistakes. No, they don't really understand everything that's going on in your school or in you. But yes, yes, yes they love you and honestly want the best things for you. And sometimes, they really might know best.

The argument with my mom about Brittany's party took place a number of years ago. (And honestly, I don't even remember what the girl's name is anymore, so I just called her Brittany.) I do remember enjoying Grandma's visit, and after I got over my sullen mood, I even had fun with my family at dinner that night. Brittany invited me to another party—which I attended and discovered she invited tons of people because she liked to be known for having big parties. She didn't care at all about being friends with me—and the party was mostly her talking about her hair . . . and nails . . . and earrings . . . and her, her, her. Very, *very* boring. And when my grandma died a few years ago, I remember wishing that we'd had more time together because I treasured those conversations with her so much.

So, all in all, Mom and Dad were right. They weren't *always* right, but they were right a lot more than I gave them credit for. (Gah! I can't believe I'm even *saying* that!)

A Few Things to Keep in Mind

1. *Tension builds on tension.* Try to come to a point of compromise or just let the issue go as soon as possible. If you're constantly arguing about the kind of music you listen to, then those fights will lead to other fights on different issues—like your friends or your schoolwork. But if you can resolve one disagreement, then you're able to start fresh with the next one. (And you're not trying to ask your parents for a favor when they're already superannoyed with you!)

2. *Show you can be responsible.* Mow the lawn if your parents ask. Study for your tests. Get to bed when you say you will. Just like Donna learned, when you prove to them that you're true to your word and what they say is important to you, they'll be more open to giving you privileges. Think of

it this way: every time you obey without complaining, make good decisions, and help out without being asked, it's like putting jelly beans in a big jar. The more full the jar gets, the more your parents will recognize that you're capable of making good decisions on your own. But every time you don't do these things, it's like taking a handful of jelly beans out.

3. *Parents don't care if "everyone" is doing something.* And more often than not, it's not true anyway. It might seem like the whole world is allowed to watch *Zombies and Werewolves in New York*, but there are plenty of kids in the same boat as you, using the same argument with *their* parents. Your family is different from any other, and especially if your parents want you to grow up with Christian values, you'll have different rules than other families have.

4. *Eighteen isn't that far away.* You won't be living with your parents forever. In a few short years, you'll be on your own. And if you want to have whipped cream and waffles for dinner and stay up until 2:00 a.m. watching movies, you'll have the freedom to do that. (Of course, you'll also have college classes to study for, a job, and bills to deal with, but I won't put a damper on your whipped-cream dream.) When I moved to my own apartment, I was pretty excited that I'd get to make my own decisions. I listened to music as loud as I wanted, painted my bedroom orange, and called my

friends after 9:00 p.m. I also could have bought those three-hundred-dollar boots if I'd wanted—but I figured Mom might have had a point about that one. (Three hundred dollars?! What was I thinking?)

5. *Parents are human.* They know what it's like to feel lonely and disappointed. They were teenagers too at one point. And even though that was back when they wore bonnets and traveled by covered wagon, they still probably remember feeling a lot of the things you do now. They're not staying up at night writing a list titled "How to Make My Daughter Miserable." (Trust me, I've checked.) Honestly, it would be easier for them to just say yes to everything—no more fights, no more complaining. But because they love you, they really and seriously want the very *best* for you long term, not just what might be fun today.

6. *You only get one set.* Not that long ago, my mom passed away. Not to make this all depressing or anything, but it really made me think. I had a lot more questions for her. I wanted her help as I decided on a career and got married and bought a house. I wanted her advice and her perspective. Because, whether I liked it or not, she knew me better than anyone else knew me. She was aware of my gifts, flaws, and needs in ways even I couldn't always see.

You might roll your eyes at this, but having a parent is a

gift—and I wish I hadn't have always taken that for granted. There aren't many people in this world who will continue to love you no matter what. Sure, Mom and Dad will get angry, irritated, and frustrated with you. And you'll get angry, irritated, and frustrated with them. But they're also the ones you will always and forever be able to call at one o'clock in the morning if there's an emergency . . . or need a place to go for Christmas. And you can count on them to dig out the photos of when you were a baby and tell the story (again!) about how you spit up on the Thanksgiving turkey. They'll remember your favorite kind of cake and believe that you can do amazing things—even when you're not so sure yourself. So take time to enjoy these years with them. Even though some days they might seem like your greatest enemies, there will come a day when they could be your closest friends.

Your Turn

Is there anything frustrating you about your parents right now? If so, you can write about it here:

_____

_____

_____

_____

_____

What are some things you really love about your parents? Write down those qualities or things they do that you'll always appreciate about them:

_____

_____

_____

_____

Keeping the things you cherish about your parents in mind, come up with some strategies to talk through your disagreements with them:

_____

_____

_____

_____

Chapter 9

Sailing on the SS Friendship

(How to Be a Good Friend)

We love our friends!

Friends will be an important part of your life these next few years. You probably already have a best friend and come across other people you connect with and really enjoy being around.

Tamika has a story about a good friend of hers.

Tamika's Corner

I met Jillian last year when we were in the same class. We both really liked dissecting frogs and ended up as lab partners. It was so fun—especially when Jillian would put on her "frog voice" and pretend the poor little amphibian was telling us his life story. She could always make me laugh. I knew a lot of girls in my class, and I would even call them friends, but I didn't have anyone I was superclose with. So when Jillian started asking me to hang out more, go to her house, or join art club together, I jumped at the chances. A few weeks later, we were inseparable.

But then I started noticing something about Jillian. She really liked to have things her way. As long as I agreed with her, we got along just fine. But whenever we disagreed, she'd get all huffy with me. (Like the time she wanted to make pottery, and I suggested we make cookies instead.) She'd put her hands on her hips and tell me my ideas were dumb. I'd usually give in and agree to do whatever she wanted to do. I mean, if it was really *that* important to her, fine. But then I started giving in a lot, all to make Jillian happy with me.

One day after leaving French club (which I didn't want to join) to meet some friends of Jillian's (who I didn't really like) to go bowling (which is my least favorite activity), I realized I didn't like being told what to do. I enjoyed Jillian as a friend, but she was incredibly bossy! I didn't know what to do . . . so I talked to my mom. She said I had three options. I could . . .

1. Look for new friends who weren't bossy.
2. Put up with Jillian's temper tantrums and keep signing up for things that *she* liked—not me.
3. Talk to her about how unhappy I was and see if she was willing to change.

I knew I had to do option number 3, but I was crazy nervous. I remember having lunch with Jillian the next day and not knowing how to start the conversation. My hands were even sweating. I pictured her stomping off and never talking to me again. But finally I gathered all my courage, took a breath, and said, "It feels like you boss me around a lot. And we only do what you like doing. It really bothers me."

She looked at me as if I'd just told her I'd given birth

to a camel. "What? Really? Me? Bossy?" I gave her a few examples. Like how much I didn't like bowling or French or pottery . . .

After a few minutes, she nodded. "I guess I never realized how pushy I can be. I really thought you were fine with all those things. I'm sorry."

I gave her a hug. Jillian didn't change right away. Even as we got up from the cafeteria table, she said, "You can throw away the trash." But then she realized she was being bossy, and she reached for the garbage.

Now she's not so bad. We're doing some activities separately, simply because I like cheerleading and she likes French club. But we're still doing a lot of things together, too. And it even seems like our friendship is stronger since that conversation!

Thanks, Tamika! There's no such thing as a perfect friend.

Friends and Friction

Penny and I have a great time together. She's a terrific person and a fun roommate, but we can really annoy each other at times. Like when I eat all of her leftover egg rolls. Or when she leaves leftovers in the fridge so long it looks like toxic sludge. We get angry at each other and say mean things sometimes. But the difference between a friendship and a really good friendship is that we talk these things out and learn from each other. We try to be better because our friendship is worth it.

You (or your friends) aren't perfect either. There will be times when you'll make mistakes: blurt out a secret, start a rumor, forget a promise. But that doesn't mean your friendship needs to be over. If you're willing to express your feelings, apologize, and forgive each other, you could be friends for a really, really long time. (Then maybe *you* can share an apartment in your early twenties and find toxic sludge in the fridge . . .)

But you might also find out your friend isn't willing to change. If she keeps breaking promises, talking about you behind your back, or doing other hurtful things, you'll need to reevaluate your friendship. It might be time to look for new friends who show you more respect. Here's a question that I hear a lot:

Q: There are "friends" who destroy each other, but a real friend sticks closer than a brother.* How do I make friends if I don't have any?

*See Proverbs 18:24.

The idea of making friends can be pretty scary. We all want friends, and we don't want to be rejected. Most of us have been in a place where we were "friend shopping," so let's hear what the girls think:

OLIVIA: "I love writing and drama, so I joined clubs and activities that girls with similar interests would be involved in too—like newspaper club and play auditions. I was able to meet a whole bunch of girls I enjoyed being around."

PENNY: "I ask a lot of questions. Seriously, I like knowing things about people. But I found out that people also really like talking about themselves. So when I ask someone about her favorite classes, or what kind of music she listens to, or what she likes to do after school, not only does it get a conversation started, but it also gives us the opportunity to see how much we have in common. Maybe she likes anchovies on her pizza, too!"

EMILY: "I discovered church is a great place to meet friends. The girls I meet there usually have similar values and beliefs, so we already have that in common. Plus, with all the group activities organized through church, I have lots of opportunities to get to know people better."

Rejection Blues

One of the downsides to having a friend is that you can lose her. There's a risk. This question from a teen girl sums up that fear:

> **Q:** My best friend is hanging out with another girl and completely ignoring me now. I've been replaced! How do I get my friend back?

You probably can't—at least not as a best friend. You could try talking to her and asking if there's something you did that hurt her. But the truth is, it's probably just time for your friendship to move on. You're both in a place of growing up and changing a *lot*. Maybe you used to play dolls together when you were little, but now you enjoy riding horses and she's into hockey. Sometimes friends change and grow in the same ways, but oftentimes these tween and teen years will move you along different paths. It can be really tough—especially when one friend is ready to move on before the other one is. It hurts to be left behind. Remember, *there's nothing wrong with you*, but young women your age simply change. You'll find new friends, probably even better friends, if you give it a little while.

In the meantime, take some extra time with Jesus. He's the best friend you'll ever have, and He's not leaving no matter how much you change. Thank Him for being a constant companion and pray that He'll lead you to the right friends.

Here's a Secret . . .

For me, learning how to be a good friend was just as tough as learning how to pick good friends. I learned about being a good friend by thinking about what I liked and didn't like in a friendship. I thought about the qualities I really liked about my friends and decided that was the kind of friend I wanted to be. It also took a lot of practice, and (unfortunately) a lot of trial and error. Just like there have been times when friends hurt me, there have been times when I've hurt my friends. Everybody makes mistakes, especially in this time of life, when we're learning what sailing on the SS *Friendship* is all about. When a hurricane hits, the best way to make the sun come out again is being humble enough to say, "I'm sorry." Learning how to say "I'm sorry" when you make a mistake and learning how to forgive are essential for friendships to thrive.

Your Turn

Remember *being* a good friend is just as important as choosing good friends. Take this quiz to see what kind of a friend you are:

1. When your friend receives the Most Valuable Player Award on the basketball team, even though you had hoped to win it, you . . .

    ☐ say congratulations and cheer louder than anyone.

    ☐ say "Great job!" but talk with other teammates about all the times she hogged the ball.

    ☐ tell her you're proud of her, but that you're kind of disappointed she didn't win it.

    ☐ give her the cold shoulder for a few days. She should know how much not getting the award hurt you.

2. When your best friend trips in the lunchroom and splashes potato soup all over her face, you . . .

    ☐ put some potato soup on your own face to get her to laugh. At least then you can share in the embarrassment with her.

    ☐ help her clean up but remind her later how embarrassing it was. You want to make sure she's more careful next time.

❑ help her get up and wipe off her face. Tell her that somebody else will trip tomorrow, and no one will remember what happened.

❑ sit down at a table far away from hers. You hope no one thinks you're as clumsy as she is.

3. When your friend tells you she's going to hang out with someone else today after school, you . . .

❑ decide you'll hang out with the new girl. She seems pretty nice too.

❑ go home and throw away everything your friend gave you. What a traitor!

❑ call her later and see if you can make plans for the weekend. Let her know that you missed hanging out with her and ask if maybe next time you could be invited too.

❑ tell everyone at school about how she still sleeps with a teddy bear. If she's going to hurt you, you're going to hurt her right back!

4. You and your BFF are at a skating party together. Suddenly she starts making fun of how you skate, and everyone starts laughing. You . . .

❑ start laughing right along with them—and replay some of your most embarrassing moments.

☐ run to the bathroom crying. You'll never talk to her again!

☐ smile and shake your head. Later you'll tell her that it was kind of embarrassing and hurt your feelings.

☐ try to change the subject by telling everyone how bad your BFF plays volleyball. Two can play at this game!

5. When your best friend tells you a secret, you . . .

☐ keep it. She trusts you, and you're not going to break that trust.

☐ don't tell anyone for a week. But then you might let it slip . . . but just to a couple other friends.

☐ ask if you can tell someone else, but when she says no, you honor your word.

☐ text a bunch of people her news after you leave. It's just too juicy not to share!

6. Your bestie gets a new haircut, and it looks terrible on her. But when she asks you what you think, you tell her . . .

☐ "I think I liked your old style a little better, but it's fun to try new things."

☐ "I love it. It's perfect on you." But then you laugh about her haircut with your other friends.

- ❑ "I like the color, but the style doesn't suit your face very well. If you want, I can help you try some different ways of styling it."
- ❑ "You look like a gorilla that's been electrocuted."

If you chose the first box, you're an upbeat person who makes for a fun friend. Just remember that it's okay to be disappointed and sad about things. Don't forget to communicate that to your friend.

If you chose the second box, you might seem like a nice friend, but you've got a chip on your shoulder. When you say one thing and do another, that's not being a true friend. Try to make sure your actions match up with your words.

If you chose the third box, you're good at communicating, which is an important part of friendship. Just remember that sometimes you might need to laugh at yourself and not take everything too seriously.

If you chose the fourth box, you tend to lean toward the selfish side. And you probably don't keep many friendships long. Try asking yourself how you would want to be treated if the roles were reversed.

CHAPTER 10

Words Can Hurt You

(How to Make Your Conversations Matter)

It started one day at lunch in sixth grade. I was sitting at the cafeteria table eating Tater Tots, and everyone around me had something important to say. Taylor was vacationing in Hawaii. Alexis
had scored the winning goal in a soccer game the day before. Ella
had bought an amazing dress. And no one was paying attention to
me. I'm not sure what made me say it, but suddenly I interrupted
everyone by blurting out, "Megan Conway got caught cheating on
her science test!"

Everyone turned to look at me, their curious eyes eager to learn more. I was instantly the center of attention. The thing is, Megan Conway might not have cheated on the test. I'd only heard a teacher ask another teacher about it. But it was probably true, right? And when I relayed the whole story, I sure made it sound that way.

I loved the attention. So every day after that, I found something else to share. Marcus Greensbro threw up on the bus. The Gatlin twins' parents were getting a divorce. And Mr. Studebaker wore a toupee.

Some of it was true, and some of it wasn't true . . . but all of it was mean.

And a week later I walked into the girls' restroom and found Megan Conway sobbing in the second stall. I asked her what was wrong—but I already knew.

"Everyone . . . everyone thinks I cheated on that science test," she told me between sniffs and hiccups. "But I didn't! I studied really, really hard for it. And . . . and the teacher believes me, but no one else does . . . and it's not true."

She blew her nose. I kicked myself in the forehead. (Well, I would have if I could have.) Instead, I took a deep breath, apologized for starting the rumor, and said, "You worked hard and you're smart. You deserved a good grade."

And then I had to go tell my table of friends the truth.

Talk about embarrassing, but I knew I had to do the right thing. The girls never believed another story of mine again. I deserved it.

"Yuck." I shoved my mom's casserole away. "This is disgusting. I'll just get some pizza at the roller rink." I pushed myself away from the dinner table and raced out the door before my parents could protest.

But I didn't miss the hurt look on my mom's face. In fact, I was still thinking about it a block from the rink. I knew my words to her had been rude and thoughtless. The casserole hadn't even been that bad—I'd just been excited to meet my friends. But Mom would understand, wouldn't she? She knew I always got excited about things. Like when I decided to enter a sculpture contest at the state fair—and made everyone eat popsicles for a month so I'd have enough to make George Washington out of the sticks. I smiled, remembering my mother looking at that horrific mass of popsicle sticks and glue on display at the fair.

"It's stunning," she'd told me, patting my head. Mom encouraged me every chance she could. Every chance. It's why I love art so much today. That hit me. I turned around to head home. Mom deserved better than my rude comments and complaining. She deserved an apology and appreciation. Skating would wait.

From Death to Life

There's a really powerful verse about words: "The tongue has the power of life and death" (Proverbs 18:21). In almost every conversation, we are speaking either life or death. Gossip, slander, and hurtful things bring death. Encouragement, hope, and truth bring life. I brought death to Megan when I said cruel things about her. I brought life to her when I apologized and complimented her.

I wish saying sorry would take the "words of death" away, but it doesn't. Once you say something, it's out there. It can't be deleted or taken back. Even six months later, I heard a girl mention that Megan Conway was a cheater, and I had to correct her. Once words are out, they spread. And you can't draw them back in. The good news is, words of life stick with us too. When Whit tells me he's proud of me or when Eugene mentions something like "I greatly admire and appreciate the fine way you connect with children at Whit's End," I'm mulling over those words for days. Sometimes I even come home and jot the words in my journal so I don't forget them.

Here's a Secret . . .

Ninety percent of your communication is nonverbal. Ninety percent! So even though I might say, "Yes, Mom!" if it's in a sarcastic or mocking tone, I'm not being as agreeable as the words imply. In fact, the tone of voice I use sometimes communicates the exact opposite of what I'm saying. Check your body language sometimes during a conversation. Are your arms and legs crossed? That communicates that you're defensive and not ready to listen to what someone else has to say. Do you roll your eyes or avoid eye contact during a disagreement? That shows dislike and disinterest. So even if you're *saying* all the right things, people are more likely to believe your nonverbal ways of communicating than what's actually coming out of your mouth. And for good reason—those behaviors are a more accurate reflection of true feelings.

And that's the kind of thing I want to come out of my mouth. I don't want my words to cause a girl to cry in the school restroom. I want to give her words that she wants to write down because they make her feel really good about herself.

So the next time you open your mouth to tell your sister you hate her, to tell the friend you're frustrated with that nobody likes her, or to tell your mom her cooking tastes like hamster food, stop. Think about it. Is it true? Is it life giving? Is it important to say? If it's not all of those things, then it's probably not worth saying.

Learning to Change

Here's a great question from a listener:

Q: It sometimes seems like my mouth starts moving before my brain catches up! How can I change?

Congratulations! The first step is wanting to change. Like everything else in life, training your tongue takes practice.

Start by putting this verse up on your mirror or in your locker as a reminder: "Don't use foul or abusive language. Let everything you say be good and helpful, so that your words will be an encouragement to those who hear them" (Ephesians 4:29, NLT).

Foul or abusive language means swearing, telling dirty jokes, yelling, saying mean things, gossiping, lying, criticizing, complaining, or calling someone a name.

Encouraging words would be Bible verses, compliments, talking kindly about others, words of inspiration and belief, or focusing on good things. Throughout the day, pause to think about what the life-giving words would be. The following chart gives you some examples. But I bet you could add in some new ones just from what happened today!

WHAT THEY SAY …	WORDS OF LIFE	WORDS OF DEATH
I have to tell you what Emma did! I can't believe how stupid she is!	You know, I'd rather not hear it. I like Emma.	Really? Give me the scoop!
Mr. Porter is the worst teacher! He hates us.	He gives a lot of homework, but I like that he offers to stay after school to help kids.	I know. Let me tell you what he did yesterday that was so mean . . .
But Mom said I could choose the show tonight!	Yeah, I got to choose yesterday. But do you mind if we watch one that we both like?	You're the worst sister in the world. I hate you!
You need to clean your room before you call anyone!	Okay, I'll do it right away. Then may I call her?	You never let me do anything I want to do!

You may think you'll be more popular if you're the one who gives the dirt on everyone. And that might make people listen to you for a few minutes. But teens know that if you're talking bad about some people, then you're probably also talking bad about *them* when they're not around. So they'll be less likely to trust you with a secret or to get too close to you, fearing they'll be your next "gossip victim." Ultimately, gossip keeps people away instead of drawing them in!

But life-giving words can grow into a friendship. When your BFF is having a rough time with something, what does she want to do? *Talk* about it, of course. So what can you say (and not say) when a friend you care about comes to you with a problem?

1. *Listen.* Sometimes it's better not to say anything at all. I can't count the number of times I just needed someone to listen and nod while I went on and on about some dilemma. Once I got all the words out, the solution seemed clearer. I really value people like Whit who ask me a lot of questions to help me figure out what to do next. But he never tells me how foolish I was for doing it in the first place (even though I probably deserved it.)

2. *Offer to help when you can.* Don't make empty promises. You're a kid, so you have a limited amount of things you can do to help. If your friend is running for class president, sure

you can offer to help with making posters. But don't tell her you'll make a hundred of them. And check with your mom first to make sure you have (or can get) the materials. One way you can help a hurting friend is to hang out with her. People feel better when they're not alone. You can also tell your friend you'll pray for her and then actually do it. And you can encourage your friend by reminding her about what a great person she is and all that she has going for her. We *all* need to hear that sometimes!

3. *Keep a secret.* This can be really hard. Sometimes we feel like we might explode because we want to tell someone else a secret. But being a good friend means keeping your promises. So if you've agreed to keep something a secret, or you know something about your friend that could be embarrassing if the word got out, keep it to yourself. (Bite your tongue if you have to.) It's a gift when someone trusts you. And it's much, much harder to rebuild trust that's been broken than to build it in the first place.

The exception to this rule is when you feel like your friend is in danger of hurting herself or someone else. If she is struggling with an eating disorder, harming herself, or talking about a plan to run away—those are things you should talk about with an adult. As kind and smart as you are, there are certain situations you simply don't have the resources to handle. If you're not sure, talk it through with your mom and/or dad to see what they think. Sometimes being a friend means protecting those close to you from their own bad decisions.

Think about some words of death you heard spoken today—even if you're the one who said them. Write them here:

_____

_____

_____

_____

_____

Now think about how you could change the words you heard or said today into life-giving words.

_____

_____

_____

_____

_____

_____

_____

_____

_____

Words begin with your thoughts. That's why God tells us in 2 Corinthians 10:5 to take every thought captive. In other words, if we control how we think, we'll be able to control what we say. The next time you hear someone speaking words of death, think about how you could respond to turn the situation into a life-giving one.

CHAPTER 11

Skip the Lip Gloss and Play Soccer

(Is Being Boy-Crazy Worth It?)

For a long time, I didn't notice boys that much. Sure, some of my friends were totally boy-*crazy*. They thought I was weird for not noticing boys, and I thought they were weird for noticing them *all* the time. I was having too much fun with my friends, and it seemed boys were only good at being loud and messy and laughing about all the noises (and smells) they could make. *Really?* I'd rather play checkers with a hamster. (They smell better too.)

But eventually some boys started to catch my eye, and I got

to know them better. Some boys came into my life because they became my friends or coworkers. I enjoyed getting to know these guys and even started to wonder if I just liked them or if I *liked* them. You know what I mean.

You'll probably get married someday. Which means, at some point, you'll go out on some dates. You're a few years away from that—and your parents are probably telling you that you're a *lifetime* away from that—but it never hurts to start thinking now about what's important to you. What are the things that you appreciate in a guy, and what are things you know for sure that you want to avoid?

Finding My Standards

If it helps, I'll tell you about some guys in my life.

The first guy I dated was named Jeff. He was nice, funny, and pretty cute, and I started to like him a lot. But eventually I had to face the fact that he wasn't a Christian. And I knew that God wanted me to marry someone who shared my faith. I had to break it off with Jeff, which was *not* fun. But I learned that in the future, I should start off a relationship knowing where a guy stands on faith issues. Is he a Christian? Does he act like it and live like it? Does he go to church and talk about how he's growing spiritually?

Eugene is a guy I never dated, but he became a good friend when we worked together at Whit's End. I have to admit, no one annoys me like Eugene sometimes does—he's kind of like a brother in that way. But I also love him to pieces because we've been through so much together. I helped him learn how to drive.* He taught me chemistry.** I gave him advice about dating his now-wife Katrina. He brought me hot chocolate when I had a bad day. With Eugene, I learned that I want to be able to have fun with whatever guy I end up marrying. I want to be able to tell him anything. I want us to be able to encourage and forgive each other. I want my husband to be my best friend.

Mitch is the guy I almost married. I saw his green eyes and went weak in the ankles. He is a strong Christian, smart, romantic, and a hard worker. He has a lot of great qualities that are important to me. So why didn't it work out? Because we were called to different things in life. He was supposed to work for the FBI, and I knew God still wanted me in Odyssey. Through that relationship, I learned to seek counsel from people close to me. Sometimes we get so blinded by how much we like someone, we don't see what's wrong with the relationship. This is when it's great to be able to talk to your parents and friends.

And I can't forget about my mentor and boss, Whit. Because my dad lives so far away and I don't have much contact with him, Whit stepped in to be that dad figure in my life. He

---

* See "A License to Drive" (episode 194, album 14).
** See "No Chemistry Whatsoever" (episode 729, album 57).

gave me advice, corrected me when I messed up, and comforted me when I needed to cry about something. I realized through Whit that I really value having someone around me who is wise, a good listener, and patient. And one thing I really appreciate about Whit is that he's a giver. He serves people—and not just ice cream! If someone has a need or a problem, he goes out of his way to help him or her.

Here's a Secret . . .

God made us girls to enjoy the attention of boys. Eve liked Adam. Rebekah was pretty impressed with Isaac. Ruth was plenty attracted to Boaz. Remember, God wrote the first love stories. He invented romance. But He also set guidelines for it because He wants you to have an amazing love story someday. For now, think about growing into who God wants you to be, as He prepares you for some beautiful relationships in the future. During this time in your life, why not be God-crazy instead of boy-crazy?

It's always good to have high standards, so that when you're ready to date, you'll be dating guys who are worth your time. But honestly, you'll have plenty of time in your life to worry and wonder about boys. Now is the time in your life to have fun with girlfriends. Make cookies, form clubs, play games, go biking, and give each other makeovers. Babysit together, try new things, and giggle over everything. Hanging out with girls can be a lot of fun! And you have a unique space in your life to do just that. Don't miss out on the opportunities you have right now.

Girls Gone Crazy

I so appreciate my girlfriends. But every once in a while, one goes gaga over a boy. What's a girlfriend to do? Here's how one listener posed the question:

It seems like more and more of my friends are getting boy-crazy! I get tired of it. Should I still hang out with them?

It can get annoying when a friend becomes fixated on one subject—or one person. It doesn't mean you have to end the friendship completely, but you should try asking her to talk about other things. Create some adventures together—go for a bike ride, write a book, start a small business, or plan a party—to get her mind off boys. There are plenty of more interesting things to talk about.

Things that don't help are watching romantic movies and reading books with romance. Those things put the lie in our heads that we're supposed to be obsessing about it. The truth is, even though relationships can make for interesting movies, our lives can be a whole lot more interesting without boys.

Camilla even has a story about that.

Camilla's Corner

Yep, I had a friend Lily, who I grew up with. We got together every Saturday to play on a soccer league at the park and always had fun together. But then tragedy struck. She went boy-crazy. And I mean seriously boy-crazy. She'd spend two hours on her hair every Saturday morning, just in case we ran into her crush, Justin. Then she'd spend another twenty minutes picking out a lip-gloss color.

"What do you think, Camilla? Pristine Peach or Raspberry Sparkle? Ooh! Or what about Magenta Dream? Hmm . . . it might be a little dark. I'm thinking Pretty-in-Pink, but I'm not sure. C'mon, Camilla! Which looks the best?"

It drove me pretty-in-pink crazy. All Lily wanted to talk about was Justin's voice, the way Justin laughed, the cute way Justin played his trumpet, and that Justin actually smiled at her the other day. (She thought; she wasn't sure. That was another debate.) Justin, Justin, Justin . . .

But what hit hardest was when she quit the soccer league.

"Sorry, Camilla," she said. "But it gets me all dirty and sweaty. Yuck! What if Justin sees me? I'd be so embarrassed!"

Well, I kept playing soccer, and Lily ended up spending more time on her hair. One Saturday, after my team won both games and I went home to drink a gallon of water, she phoned dirty-and-sweaty little me.

"Wanna go to the mall tonight and hang out?" Lily asked.

"Sure," I told her. "I'll just check with my mom. Why do you want to go?"

"I heard Justin was going to be there! He's going to a

movie with some of his friends. Maybe we can go see *The Attack of the Slime-Covered Mushrooms* too!"

That's where I drew the line. No monster mushroom movies! But I did miss hanging out with Lily, so after my mom agreed, I told Lily I'd meet her at the mall.

We actually had a pretty fun time that evening, once she stopped craning her neck every thirty seconds to see if Justin was nearby. But then, it happened. A crowd of boys from school emerged from the movie theater, loudly imitating what a slimy mushroom might sound like if it attacked the world.

"There he is! There he is!" Lily squealed. She smoothed her top, ran her fingers through her perfectly styled hair, and hurriedly applied some Pristine Peach lip gloss. "How do I look? Is there anything in my teeth?"

I assured her there wasn't.

But then it got worse. Justin looked over our way and started *walking toward us*. I knew the rest of the time at the mall would be miserable. If they had a conversation, Lily would be talking about it for the next two hours. And what if he wanted to walk around with us? I groaned out loud.

Justin wore a big smile as he came closer. But he wasn't smiling at Lily. He was smiling at . . . *me*!

"Hi! You're Camilla, right?"

"Um, yeah. This is my friend Lil—"

"I was in the park today watching my sister play soccer in the league. That goal you scored at the end of the second period was awesome!"

"Oh . . . uh, thanks!"

"Sure. I'll probably see you next week!"

And with that, he turned and walked away.

Lily stared after him. "He didn't even look at me," she muttered. "My lip-gloss color doesn't matter at all."

Lily spent the night, and we were able to have a good talk. I told her I felt like time with her was sometimes wasted because she was always concerned about how she looked, where the boys were, and what everyone thought of her. I said she was just not fun anymore. I think this time she really understood.

More to Life

That's the problem with boy-craziness: when it becomes so much of a focus that all we care about is getting noticed by boys, we miss out on who we really are. Some girls start thinking about changing to become what a certain boy might like and then stop doing other things they enjoy. What a waste!

It's great if you think a boy is nice, or notice that he has a great sense of humor or a cute smile. But it's nothing worth getting obsessed about. Your life is full of too many fun activities and possible friends to build your schedule around getting attention from a boy you'll most likely hardly remember in a couple weeks.

Your Turn

Think about your dad (or dad-like substitute), brother, and guy friends. What are some qualities that you appreciate about them that you'd hope for in a future spouse?

_____

_____

_____

_____

_____

Now think about some qualities you definitely *don't* want in a future spouse. Like I learned from my relationship with Jeff, knowing what you don't want can be just as important as knowing what you do want.

_____

_____

_____

_____

Now that you have your standards set, you'll be ready for dating when the time comes. Until then, take this important time in your life to learn more about who God created *you* to be!

Start an adventure!
with Focus on the Family

Whether you're looking for new ways to teach young children about God's Word, entertain active imaginations with exciting adventures or help teenagers understand and defend their faith, we can help. For trusted resources to help your kids thrive, visit our online Family Store at: